Waking the Women

Waking the Women

*Faith, Menopause and the
Meaning of Midlife*

Jayne Manfredi

CANTERBURY
PRESS
Norwich

© Jayne Manfredi 2024

Published in 2024 by Canterbury Press
Editorial office
3rd Floor, Invicta House,
110 Golden Lane
London EC1Y 0TG, UK
www.canterburypress.co.uk

Canterbury Press is an imprint of Hymns Ancient & Modern Ltd
(a registered charity)

Hymns Ancient & Modern® is a registered trademark of
Hymns Ancient & Modern Ltd
13A Hellesdon Park Road, Norwich,
Norfolk NR6 5DR, UK

Scripture quotations are from New Revised Standard Version Bible:
Anglicized Edition, copyright © 1989, 1995 National Council of
the Churches of Christ in the United States of America. Used by
permission. All rights reserved worldwide.

British Library Cataloguing in Publication data

A catalogue record for this book is available
from the British Library

ISBN 978-1-78622-575-7

Typeset by Regent Typesetting

Contents

To my mum Jackie, who showed me the way.
To Marianna, who travels with me.
And to my daughters Jana and Lyla,
who will follow in our footsteps.

Acknowledgements

Writing a book can feel like a lonely undertaking; for so much of the process it's just you and your laptop screen. But even the idea for this book itself didn't emerge without the help of willing collaborators, who recognized and valued the need for an awakening in the church around the issue of menopause. *Waking the Women* began with the storytelling and sharing of wisdom and worries of the women who messaged me, talked with me, sent me lengthy emails, and filled in my questionnaires. You know who you all are. We said we needed the church to talk about menopause and so we did. Thank you.

Thank you to Alison Fenton and Barbara Glasson, my tutors at The Queen's Foundation in Birmingham, who both encouraged me to write and gave me the confidence to do it. Thank you also to Michael Gayle, librarian extraordinaire, for patience and kindness in the face of my repeated tardiness and general ineptitude. Thank you to Debbie Young-Somers for answering my questions and for generally just being awesome. A special thank you to David Shervington, my commissioning editor, whose belief in me and championing of my writing made this book possible, and genuinely helped save my life.

When you're staring at that laptop screen it can feel like a Sisyphean task, but there were, of course, people who helped shoulder that burden, and for that I'm eternally grateful. Thank you to my holy encourager and fierce champion the Revd Sam Maginnis who picked me up and held me there so that I could write, and to Andrew Graystone for his support of me and this book. Thank you to Marianna, who prayed with me, encouraged me, walked with me, advised me, and read every word almost as soon as I wrote it. I couldn't have done it without you.

To Leonardo, who cajoled/consoled/supported/blackmailed me into writing using coffee as leverage. *You know.* And to Jana, Lyla, Rafael and Lorenzo: thank you for keeping me awake so I can help wake the women. I love you.

A postcard from the wilderness 1

If you've picked up this book, I'm assuming it's because you're perimenopausal, planning on being at some point, or you've already gone through menopause. Perhaps you've picked it up because you love someone who is going through this life stage, and you want to know how best to support them. Or maybe you're one of my friends and are reading it because I've threatened you. Either way, I need to give you a few heads up before we start our journey. First, I need to prepare you by just coming straight out and saying that vaginal dryness is one of the topics that we'll discuss. Menopause is not for the squeamish and you need to know what you're getting into from the off.

My focus is Christian women of faith who are middle-aged and are either experiencing perimenopause or are already menopausal. It's done with a respect for the diverse and multifarious lives of women and their experiences of menopause, but also with an appreciation of my own limitations. Some reflections will resonate deeply. Some may not. It's my prayer that everyone who reads this will see the value in me publicly naming experiences that have for so long been a source of silent shame. I feel comforted that even feminist theologian and poet Nicola Slee, who has written so boldly and courageously about women and our bodies, has also admitted how she's struggled at times to fully own her voice as a woman.[1] Our journey into the wilderness of menopause still feels like taboo territory.

Womanhood is subject to simplistic stereotypes and endless binaries that attempt to police our options, limit our choices, and seek to divide us: whore versus virgin. Married versus single. Children versus childless. Young versus old. Vaginal birth versus caesarean birth. Bottle versus breast. Work versus stay at home. Ageing *gracefully* versus *getting work done*. Good versus bad, right versus wrong, holy versus unholy, the false dichotomies are endless. Throughout my life I've felt judged for the things I've done or not done and for the choices I've made or not made. This has included everything from only having one child ('selfish') to then having three more ('breeder'), to my preference for high heels ('not feminist'), red lipstick ('tarty'), fondness for pints of beer ('not ladylike'), and that time I had my hair shorn off into a pixie cut ('probably getting divorced' and 'recently become a lesbian'). If I've learned anything at all, it's that I can't win, no matter what I do, but if what's meant by winning is universal, bland approval, then I'd rather lose and be free to make my own choices without reference to what anyone else thinks. More about this freedom to lose later!

If you're labouring under the assumption menopause is a time of unity and universal solidarity for women, then I'm sorry to disappoint. It's a topic that's just as divisive as anything else when it comes to women and our bodies. Hormone therapy versus cold turkey. 'A natural process' versus 'a hormone deficiency'. 'We need to talk about this' versus 'wasn't a big deal in my day, and we coped just fine'.

Menopause is an incendiary subject for lots of women, triggering feelings of anger and frustration, and in some cases, outright despair. I'm aware that some women enter conversations about menopause after having been ignored by their doctors and marginalized in their workplace. They feel shunned by the church and misunderstood by their families. I've learned that some women have developed very strong feelings about how best to meet their needs during menopause, and that the church alone isn't going to measure up, which is why you won't find a partisan approach to menopause here. My goal isn't to tell you how you ought to tackle it to cope with potential symptoms. My hope is to explore how God might feel about menopause, and to offer some comfort and solidarity along the way. I wholeheartedly endorse your choice to use hormone therapy if that's what you need, and I also offer my support if that route isn't for you. The God who gave us free will has respect for our choices, and one way for us to love and honour each other during this life phase is to do the same.

It's my hope that my words will be read with the kind of intellectual humility and curiosity that's so often lacking in online discourse. This is a journey undertaken together, and in close proximity to one another. We're bound to push each other's buttons and grind one another's gears, but as St Paul said, love isn't rude and it doesn't insist on its own way (1 Corinthians 13). He also said it's not irritable either, but he never suffered with hormonal rage so bad he could punch a baby capybara in the throat, so let's just take it one step at a time, OK? We can't always be Christlike.

In researching menopause, I've tried to include as many perspectives as possible, from as wide a range of sources as possible. This book has still been written by me, a woman situated in a particular time and place with experiences that are unique to me and me alone. I'm also not kidding when I say I'm deeply flawed, because I so am. I humbly ask for your charity if I fail to shine enough of a light on experiences and perspectives that aren't my own. I'm hoping this book will serve as a prompt for you to explore further or develop the boldness to tell your own story. My words are just one handful of seed thrown on a garden that will cultivate many other women's stories. So many that the church can no longer deny, by ignorance or by deliberate fault, that what happens to women is the kingdom business of us all.

The Revd Jayne Manfredi
Crewe, Epiphany 2024

Note

1 Slee, N., 'Writing like a Woman: In search of a feminist theological poetics', in D'Costa, G., et al., *Making Nothing Happen: Five Poets Explore Faith and Spirituality* (Farnham: Ashgate, 2014).

We set off on our journey

'Where you go, I will go.'

Ruth 1.16–17

Come, little sisters, daughters and friends. Come, older sisters, mothers and aunties. Come, grandmothers and older women of wisdom.

Come.

Let's follow Naomi and her daughter-in-law Ruth as they travel together from Moab and into the unknown together. Let me be your guide. We are not alone. Let's be a place of refuge and sanctuary for one another. Let's listen to each other cry and make one another laugh. This is our journey.

Come, my daughters. You are in a wilderness all your own, one created by the hormonal upheaval of puberty. Unsure of yourself and uncomfortable in the body that was once yours to dance and move with the freedom that your brothers still enjoy. Now it feels like it's the property of the world; on display and scrutinized by hungry and critical eyes, none more so critical than your own.

Come, my little sister. You're still far away from this desert of unknowing, but you're a woman and so it's your destiny. You're a slave to a twenty-eight-day cycle, your body no longer your own. Maybe you will create new life. Maybe you won't. I know you'll be judged either way. I know some of your struggles. I know the pain of fertility failed. The distress of miscarriage and the joy of new life. I know the alien feel of a pregnant body and the bruised and wounded post-partum one. I know there is more to you than just being a mum.

Come, my friend. Let's journey together into this unchartered moment; not young any more but not yet old. I know what it's like to see those first grey hairs and those lines, like cracks in fine porcelain. To not be the woman you once were and the struggle to cope with changes that our culture sees as flaws. I sometimes feel like I've lost myself – do you feel it too? I know what it's like to feel unexplained rage followed by implacable sadness. To toss and turn at night with mysterious aches and pains. This is the liminal space of our womanhood, and so much is unknown and uncertain. Let's be company for one another as we travel through change.

Come, my mother. Help me to cross over the threshold. You've travelled this way before. You made it. Show me the way. Tell me the lessons you learned while you travelled. Were you ministered to by angels and did you wrestle with beasts? Did you have challenging conversations with demons? Tell me what was manna to you along the road. Share your wisdom with me and I will pass it back down the line to those who stand on the borderland of this wilderness space, and back further, to those who won't make it here for many years to come. But come they will.

Let's leave words as crumbs on the pathway for them to follow. Let's leave our witness and tell our stories. This wilderness has places that are barren. Sometimes we might need to climb. Sometimes we might fall into unseen pits. We might lose our way. Let's carve on a rockface of this unfamiliar wasteland to declare to those who follow that *God was here*.

Take my hand.

Let's journey together.

I

Church, I say to you, arise

'Sleeper, awake! Rise from the dead,
and Christ will shine on you.'

Ephesians 5.14

I'm preaching online at an Oxford college. I have my notes up on the screen; carefully and meticulously researched, written and re-written. I don't wear make-up regularly, but I'm wearing it now; expertly and carefully applied, because this will be recorded, and the internet lives for ever. Preaching to myself on a laptop screen is the most unnatural thing; I want to concentrate on the sentences I've painstakingly crafted, on the words laboriously translated from the ancient Greek using a dictionary and zero knowledge of biblical languages. But for some reason my mind wants to focus only on my agile and cartoonishly large face, as it pontificates at me on the screen, a recurring and immovable thought refusing to be dislodged:

Oh my God, am I getting jowls?

Don't judge me. I'm forty-five. It's an unforgiving and disconcerting age for a woman to be. If you've not hit middle-age yet then you can't possibly know the horror of opening up your phone and accidentally being assaulted by the image on your front-screen camera – there she is: your baffled face, hanging there like a Shar Pei. At times like these you might be tempted to lie to yourself and blame the camera angle or the poor quality of your phone. As your fellow sufferer, I would encourage you in these deceptions. It's a great coping mechanism, as is wearing a scarf to disguise that other middle-aged affliction that I like to call 'Random Tortoise Neck'. This is a disease that only shows itself when you're least expecting it; in the mirror your neck might look perfectly serviceable. Lithe even. Dare I say it, youthful. Then, bam! You're on a Zoom call or someone takes a photo of you unexpectedly, and there is your tortoise neck. Where did that crepey, stretched-out, ugly skin come from? It's very distressing.

If you're reading this and are now thinking of rushing to the nearest mirror to scrutinize your own throat, I feel duty bound to inform you that Random Tortoise Neck is, unfortunately, just the tip of the midlife iceberg. In a recent conversation with my best friend, she lamented the fact that none of her beloved, best summer skirts fit her any more, and she'd had to pass them on to her slimmer, younger sister. This is a woman who has never been bigger than eight stone wet-through at nine months pregnant and is still objectively very slim. But there is no denying that for most women, as we age, like Shakira's hips, our midriffs can't lie. Depleting levels of oestrogen in our bodies cause us to lay down visceral fat and this is sadly deposited round our middles, announcing loudly that our bodies are on the change and on the move, mostly outwards and down towards our feet.

When I was a kid, this seemingly unenviable life period between the ages of approximately forty-five and fifty-five was actually known as *The Change*. Germaine Greer wrote a whole book about it: she called menopause 'the invisible Rubicon that a woman cannot know she is crossing until she has crossed it'.[1] This was back in 1991. Things must be different for women now, *surely?*

Well, yes ... and no. The last few years have seen menopause[2] activism develop almost as a cottage industry, with UK celebrities including Davina McCall,[3] Mariella Frostrup,[4] Andrea McLean,[5] Meg Matthews,[6] and many others, all offering their own testimonies of their midlife experiences. You can listen to a dozen different podcasts all discussing the challenges of depleting hormone levels. Menopause is everywhere and sometimes I worry we've hit critical mass. When I tell some people about my own research on menopause and faith, their eyes glaze over in a similar manner as if I've asked them if they want to see photos from my holiday in Lloret de Mar. The message from some quarters seems to be *enough already*; Mr Bennet has

walked purposely over to us, hot and sweating at the piano-
forte (probably mid hot flush) and said, 'That will do extremely
well, child. You have delighted us long enough. Let the other
young ladies have time to exhibit.'[7] The stress being on the
word *young*, of course.

Before we exit the parlour, let's first take stock of how all
the celebrity activism in the secular world has impacted the
Christian world of church and faith, as that is what this book
is about after all. This is the world I inhabit; although frankly,
as a deacon I straddle both worlds. According to the liturgy
from my ordination, deacons are heralds of Christ's kingdom.
In other words, it's literally our job to shout about God. We
serve the communities in which we live and then we bring back
to the church the needs of the people we've served. The deacon
is a bridge between the world and the church:

> They are to work with their fellow members in searching out
> the poor and weak, the sick and lonely and those who are
> oppressed and powerless, reaching into the forgotten corners
> of the world, that the love of God may be made visible.[8]

I'm living out my diaconal calling: I'm grabbing a torch, getting
down on my hands and knees, and reaching into the corners of
the church to shine a light on an area of women's lives which
is as forgotten as a Thigh Master gathering dust in a bedroom.
While the secular world has been enjoying a menopause boom,
the conversation within the church has barely even begun.

Pentecostal writer, pastor and teacher Cheryl Bridges Johns,
whose book *The Seven Transforming Gifts of Menopause* has
proved to be an oasis of knowledge and empowerment in a
church echoing with silence on the lives of older women, writes:

> The Church pretty much follows the pattern of the larger
> society in ignoring the lifelong journey of women. Women
> at mid-life are expected to be the same as they were in young
> adulthood. The Church offers few safe places for anger, and
> no support groups for women during perimenopause. There
> are no rites of passage for women, and no ways of honouring
> older, post-menopausal women as elders.[9]

It's a depressingly accurate assessment. I discovered, while attempting to write about menopause and faith during my ministerial training, that there is still very little theological research on this topic.

In the UK and America, there is a significant gender gap in our churches, with women making up the majority of church-goers.[10] The age gap in the church is also well known and documented (for example, statistics for the Church of England indicate that congregants over the age of forty-five vastly outnumber the young).[11] It is unfathomable to me that peri-menopause and menopause are not spoken about or referenced in our churches when the majority of people in them are either going through it or have experienced it.

I took to social media to see if any of the women of faith whom I'm connected with would be interested in meeting for an online chat about it. I was *inundated* with replies. The overwhelming response was one of relief.

'Thank you so much for starting this conversation!'

'No one in the church talks about this; it's so taboo.'

As I started to talk to more midlife and older women, that word – *taboo* – cropped up again and again. Women talked of not being heard, not feeling seen, not being understood or fully recognized. They expressed feelings of despondency and loneliness at having their interior lives go unacknowledged. There was an overarching frustration to lots of responses that named the church's ignorance of issues affecting women's bodies and its historic refusal to publicly voice and honour our bodily processes. An underlying resentment and disturbing dissonance that a life phase they were finding all-encompassing and far-reaching was completely ignored.

Considering that women are the dominant demographic in churches, these are surprising comments to make. Clearly, in a very real and practical sense, women *are* being heard in our churches: in our pulpits, in our home groups, at our altars, at the church porch and in the pews. Women are present and are vital to the mission and ministry of the church. We *are* talking but, clearly, certain things just aren't being said.

The celebrity-driven, public conversation about perimenopausal symptoms is waking the world up to the physical reality of women's lives. Women are becoming more knowledgeable about the process, of signs to look out for and symptoms to be aware of. Menopause is no longer the invisible Rubicon that Germaine Greer identified; if you're over the age of forty, you can't help but be aware of it now. This is mostly a good thing! Awareness empowers us to visit our GP and to advocate for ourselves and each other, to share knowledge and advice. These are vital conversations for everyone to hear, including male partners, colleagues and friends. Being aware of how best to support women through this life stage, should they need it, is crucial. Implementing this information to put into place workplace policies or to just have a greater understanding of what a woman might be experiencing during her perimenopausal years, and the impact this could have on her, is a positive step for women. It all contributes towards the greater good of destigmatizing our bodies and the experience of being female. This is God's good work and is something the church absolutely ought to be concerning itself with.

I've listened to women, and I've learned that for many of them accessing good care and treatment is vital. They reported so much more than the hot flushes that we associate with perimenopause: unrelenting insomnia, brain fog, crippling anxiety, loss of sense of self and isolation, loneliness and feelings of inexplicable rage. It's a time in life where these debilitating symptoms collide with reaching an age where women are increasingly regarded as having outlived our welcome in terms of our value to society. If you're a mother, it often coincides with facing the empty nest, or if you're not, a woman must contend anew with the death-knell finality that menopause presents them with. This might be especially painful or it might even be a relief. In a practical sense, after menopause women are no longer reproductively useful, and so older women represent a challenge to patriarchal norms that see human bodies as reaching adulthood and remaining unchanging: 'A male-default understanding of progress and change, one in which the loss of one's reproductive prowess is meant to signify a form of death.'[12] This lands hard in a church context, where patriarchal norms of motherhood and family are pervasive and largely unchanging.

I don't want to add to anyone's frustration or sense of not being heard, because my mission is that women feel listened to and respected. I want to assert that God cares about your pain and your experiences. But I want so much more for us than just awareness raising so we can alleviate symptoms. I want *all* women to be affirmed in their ageing, an experience that adds to our value as beloved children of God, not takes away. Something that speaks of giftedness not weakness or debilitation.

A Christian response to menopause would be mindful of the consequences of the language we use to describe our experiences. Susan Mattern writes, in *The Slow Moon Climbs*: 'To speak of oestrogen deficiency is to say that women past menopause do not have as much oestrogen as they ideally should; in this view women of reproductive age set the standard for the right amount of oestrogen.'[13] This is a really important point. A responsible, wise and loving Christian ethic of menopause would not frame it as a hormone deficiency, thereby casting menopausal women as defective. Some of the urgency in raising awareness of perimenopausal symptoms, legislatively and for therapeutic purposes, has meant that, inadvertently, older women and women who are unable to take HRT for medical reasons have been thrown under the bus. We should be free to make our own choices about what care we choose to seek to alleviate symptoms that for some of us might feel unbearable. But I don't think this freedom ought to come at the expense of denigrating our older sisters, or in the process, circuitously dunking on ourselves. After all, we will all be old women eventually, God willing.

Our older sisters, who have already been through perimenopause and out the other side, have so much to teach us about what they learned. Many of them have noted that when they were going through the perimenopause, it was an off-limits topic entirely, not discussed publicly, let alone in churches. They became middle-aged in a church that resolutely refused to acknowledge that they were women at all (in any physical sense) and the pressure to conform to a male standard of ministry was huge. I've had conversations with women who navigated the challenges of being among the first few cohorts of women priests in the Church of England in the mid-1990s, and part of that challenge included the necessity to prove that being a woman was no barrier to exercising priestly ministry. Acknowledging publicly, via liturgy, prayer or preaching, that there might be inherent difficulties and obstacles that are germane to a female embodied state, would have been unspeakable.

Women are still fearful of admitting that our bodies function in particular ways lest our differences be perceived as limiting us just because we digress from a perceived male norm. Our male counterparts, whose bodies, largely unchanging and static and not subject to the inconvenience of cyclical upheaval, are still seen as the default way of being human, with women's bodies reduced to a sub-category. The pressure to fit into a priestly role where the standard is male has undoubtedly inhibited women from exploring what ministry – and the church – could look like if we expanded the horizons of what it means to be priestly; *in persona Christa*, not just *Christi*.

What would it mean for the church if women fully owned their embodied experiences, without shame, without embarrassment, without apology? This is the church I want for my daughters and for myself. I want it for anyone who has a body with needs that the church ought to be recognizing, or with a body that presents a direct challenge to traditional norms: churches with poor access for wheelchairs, inadequate toilet facilities and plumbing, enforced ableist conventions such as standing to sing or kneeling to pray, these things are just the start of that recognition. A church that declares emphatically and without equivocation that bodies are important, would be gloriously incarnational. It would benefit us all.

Divesting the church of its squeamishness of women's bodies is the mission I've chosen to accept. How God sees my body, my mother's body, my daughter's body, *your body* is deeply relevant to our Christian tradition. We worship a God who chose to be broken for us by first breaking the body of a woman. The soft, boneless fontanelle of Jesus' head burst through membranes, splashing fluid and stretching flesh to *literally* break into a world where he would be broken, again and again, for broken people. Breaking bodies are absolutely integral to our shared Christian story. What happens to women over a life-tide matters to God and it matters to the church. 'Storylessness, after all, has been women's big problem.'[14] Menopause is an inescapable and important part of our story. We need to tell it.

God says to Isaiah:

> even to your old age I am he,
>> *even when you turn grey I will carry you.*
> I have made, and I will bear;
>> I will carry and will save. (Isaiah 46.4)

I read something more in my Bible than what I am seeing in current newspaper articles, 'inspiring' Instagram posts, or hearing on the latest celebrity podcast episode. My faith tells me that what God has made and declared good stays good, even if the world does all it can to convince us it's not. Dear reader, you may have listened to the latest celebrity podcast about menopause (it's probably called *Hot Flushes are the New Hot*, or something similar) and you may have felt inspired and empowered by it. I hold my hands up and confess I'm tired by much of the current discussion about menopause. There's a desperation to some of the conversation which wants to not so much walk beside women as they age, but to deny that it's happening at all. 'Older women can still slay!' they defiantly claim. Do I really have to still slay? *Still?* 'Age doesn't have to be something unattractive.'[15] What if I want the freedom to not care about being attractive any more?

I want to suggest a glimpse of something more than that. I see menopause as having the potential for freedom not because I will still *have it*, whatever that elusive *it* might be, but because I won't need to have it any more. The culturally imposed rules we apply to women such as unattainable beauty standards, restrictive feminine norms, or limiting stereotypes based upon our reproductive capabilities – or perceived lack of – become less of an issue as you age because all of those poten-tial drag-factors are linked to being young, and if there's one thing you won't be any more after you hit forty, it's young. All the hormone therapy, hair dye or skin smoothing and plumping creams in the world won't change that. We must contend with a new reality. Celebrity-driven menopause often looks a lot different to how it might look for me, or you, or any of the other women of humble and obedient faith I've spoken to. What does menopause look like as seen through the eyes of God? That's the question that most interests me and what this book is an attempt to explore.

I recognize a thirst and a hunger in middle-aged women of faith; we aren't content any more to be silent and accept the stones the church gives us. We want understanding. Acknowledgement. Affirmation. Respect. We want bread. Like Miriam, we are grabbing tambourines, handing them out and making a racket together. Like the quickening in Elizabeth's menopausal belly, we are stirring and we're waking up the church. We are banging our tambourines and we're declaring that just like Elizabeth, just like Sarah, older women can be the repositories of new life and possibility. It's happening just like God planned. Menopausal bodies matter: they are not deficient. They too are women's bodies. Fearfully and wonderfully made. Our stories matter.

Your story matters.

You're not depleting and decaying like a uranium rod; year by year the strength and core of you fading. The essence of you isn't diminishing. God says: *Even though you are changing, I am still the same. When your jawline is jowly and your neck is crepey, when your hair is greying and your middle is spreading, when your brain is forgetful, when the bleeding stops and you don't know yourself as you once did, you will still be known by me. I will carry you and I will save.*

This isn't *The Change.*

It's an evolution.

Notes

1 Greer, G., *The Change: Women, Ageing and the Menopause* (London: Bloomsbury, 2019, revised edition, p. 22).

2 We tend to use the word menopause to denote the entire life period, when in reality we mean the perimenopause, the period of declining hormones and associated symptoms which leads to the menopause, a word used to describe the state when menstruation has permanently ceased. This is defined by no bleeding for twelve months. If menopause is the destination, then perimenopause is the journey. Katerina Wilk, in *Perimenopower: Your Essential Guide to the Change Before the Change* (London: Orion Spring, 2020), defines perimenopause as 'The time before your final period when hormonal changes are experienced. It can start as early as thirty-five, but for most women it begins between the ages of forty and forty-five.' I'll sometimes use menopause and perimenopause interchangeably, because colloquially this probably makes the most sense to people.

3 McCall, D. with Potter, N., *Menopausing: The Positive Roadmap to Your Second Spring* (London: HarperCollins, 2022).

4 Frostrup, M. and Smellie, A., *Cracking the Menopause While Keeping Yourself Together* (London: Bluebird, 2021).

5 McLean, A., *Confessions of a Menopausal Woman: Everything You Wanted to Know but Were Afraid to Ask* (London: Bantam Press, 2018).

6 Matthews, M., *The New Hot: Taking on the Menopause with Attitude and Style* (London: Vermillion, 2020).

7 Austen, J., *Pride and Prejudice* (London: Penguin Classics, first published in 1813, this edition 1996).

8 The Archbishops' Council, 'Ordination of Deacons', in *Common Worship: Ordination Services* (London: Church House Publishing, 2020).

9 'Interview: Cheryl Bridges Johns, Professor of Spiritual Renewal', talking to Terence Handley MacMath, *The Church Times*, 23 October 2020, https://www.churchtimes.co.uk/articles/2020/23-october/features/interviews/interview-cheryl-bridges-johns-professor-of-spiritual-renewal (accessed 26.4.24).

10 Trzebiatowska, M. and Bruce, S., *Why are Women More Religious than Men?* (Oxford: Oxford University Press, 2012). Statistics quoted include data from United Reformed, Baptist, Anglican, Methodist, Presbyterian, Roman Catholic and 'other' Christian churches, and no denomination.

11 Curtice, J., Clery, E., Perry, J., Phillips M. and Rahim, N. (eds), 'British Social Attitudes: The 36th Report' (London: The National Centre for Social Research, 2019).

12 Smith, V., *Hags: The Demonisation of Middle-Aged Women* (London: Fleet, 2023, p. 78).

13 Mattern, S., *The Slow Moon Climbs: The Science, History and Meaning of Menopause* (Princeton: Princeton University Press, 2019).

14 Pollitt, Katha, 'Forword', in Heilbrun, Carolyn G., *Writing and Women's Life* (New York: W.W. Norton & Company, 1988, p. xvi).

15 Wilk, K., *Perimenopower: Your Essential Guide to the Change Before the Change* (London: Orion Spring, 2020, p. 31).

We make camp on the first night

From menarche to menopause

I sit by the fire, nimble fingers at work with wool and hook, steadily looping yarn in the hope of making something beautiful, and I think about my daughters. Silently, I weave a prayer of blessing around their heads, these two beautiful girls whom God knitted together in my womb. There are so many images of God. The potter. The gardener. The warrior. My most treasured image is God the Yarnist. I like to picture the one who crafted the universe with knobbly, arthritic fingers clutching chunky needles and fluffy mohair thread, patiently muttering 'pearl one, knit one', to himself, as creation unfurls onto his lap and down to the ground, all the way into existence. But I digress.

Women are warming their hands on enamel mugs of tea, their smooth and weathered faces lit in flickering shades of orange and gold. They are individuals, all with their own unique stories to tell, but just like the burgeoning blanket, which covers my lap as I patiently stitch, the story of our lives is woven together by common threads. We are bound by bodies that bleed – those who have just begun, those who bleed with accustomed familiarity, those whose wombs are just beginning to stutter, and those for whom the bleeding is a distant memory. We are Sarah. We are Naomi. We are Elizabeth. We are Anna.

But there's someone missing from the campfire. She was too young to make the journey, but she begged to come along with her big sisters. Weary after a full day in the wilderness, she lies under the stars, lulled to sleep by the gentle conversation of the women nearby. She is Eve before the snake; her naked innocence and honest thirst for life, absent of embarrassment, awkwardness or shame. Soon enough she will meet snakes and eat bad fruit, just like the rest of us did. Her life is an Eden where the bleeding hasn't yet begun.

Our time has been marked by drops of blood. It first came when we weren't expecting it and made a mess in our clothes. It didn't come when it was supposed to, forcing us to wait in tearful frustration and rage, scrutinizing the calendar, counting and recounting days, praying for the relief that it brought. Then it came when we didn't want it to. It spoiled things. Special occasions. Days out. Holidays. Sports. It came when it felt like it. It came regularly, and without fail. It sometimes destroyed our hopes and dreams. It took away possibility. It washed away new life. It brought everything from a bloated tummy, painful and unsightly pimples, to agonizing cramping pains and an indescribable yearning for chocolate. It cleansed us from within and allowed us to start again. It caused embarrassment. It helped us make friends with women we didn't know in public loos. It underscored the rhythm of our adult lives and it did this so pervasively that we forgot who we were before it all began. We forgot who we were before the bleeding started.

It's time to go and wake her up.

2

While we were sleeping

'This girl isn't dead. She's sleeping.'
Matthew 9.23–26[1]

My daughter started her periods during the first Covid-19 lock-down in 2020. This really added to the joy of all six of us being incarcerated with one another twenty-four seven, I can tell you. The poor mite cried her heart out for days, as her tiny body bled copiously and without ceasing, accompanied by the kind of twisting cramps that feel as if your uterus is being wrung out to dry. She cried because of the pain, but mostly she cried because of the blood – the volume of it, the relentlessness of it, the wet, sticky, unwelcome discomfort of it. She cried because we'd ordered a bouncy castle for her brother's birthday, and she was unable to join in with the jumping and the fun. She was eleven years old.

Can you remember how it was before the bleeding started? We climbed trees. We went swimming whenever we felt like it. We rough-housed and play fought and did handstands and cartwheels, relishing in the use of our limbs. We didn't worry that our knickers were on show. We didn't need to worry about underwiring. We bared our bony chests without shame, and nobody ogled us or wolf whistled or told us we were being *too revealing* or showing *too much skin*. Our flesh was as neutral as that of our brothers, exciting neither admiration nor condem-nation. We were free in a way we wouldn't be after the bleeding started. We owned our own voice and we used it to say what we meant and ask for the things we needed. We didn't apolo-gize all the time. We could put ourselves first without feeling bone-deep guilt. We could walk past a building site without bending our heads and folding ourselves inwards, trying to disappear. We enjoyed our food without remorse, and we took up as much space as we needed to take. We believed in magic and we knew we had the power to slay our own dragons, because we were as strong and as brave as our brothers and we knew it to the tips of our toes. What the hell happened?

To re-purpose the now dated phrase Germaine Greer used when she published her book in 1991, *The Change* does indeed happen to women, but I want to suggest that another, in some ways far more catastrophic and disruptive change takes place when we are still little more than children, because I believe so much of the mental stress of menopause – the doubt, the confusion, the rage, the despair – has deep roots that reach far back into our past. Cheryl Bridges Johns describes female puberty as a time of self-censoring, the beginning of the loss of real self:

> Many of us stifled our true voice sometime in adolescence, when we were more concerned with fitting in, finding our place, and following the rules.[2]

This First Change is our metamorphosis from our wild, spontaneous pre-pubescent selves, unencumbered by societal expectations or restrictions, to female adolescents, with bodies that feel publicly owned, exposed and in need of taming. According to Bridges Johns, we lost our authentic self. She was washed away by a deluge of hormones and stereotypical expectations of what constitutes a woman, which restricted who we were made by God to be. This is something I've observed happen in my own daughters, in myself and in my friends.

In their ground-breaking research study, *Meeting at the Crossroads: Women's Psychology and Girl's Development*, psychologists Lynn Mikel Brown and Carol Gilligan explore the relationship between girls and women, and try to discover what happens to girls on the journey to womanhood. After working with a group of one hundred girls between the ages of seven and eighteen for five years, they identify a series of psychologically wounding disconnections, 'between psyche and body, voice and desire, thoughts and feelings, self and relationship'.[3]

They began studying women's psychological development

by first listening to the voices of women and comparing them to the voices of men. The differences were stark: men spoke as self-governing, autonomous creatures, 'free to speak and move as they pleased',[4] existing independently of their relationships, whereas the women identified a clear loss of voice and self-sacrifice for the sake of connection to others. This is also something that many women who are perimenopausal confess to feeling; a sense of a loss of self and a frustration at not being heard. Just as perimenopause is a borderland[5] and a liminal space between life stages, so too is adolescence. The researchers observed that girls during this time lost their 'vitality, their resilience, their immunity to depression, their sense of themselves and their character'.[6]

This is all horribly familiar, and not just because we've been here before. One of the most common refrains I've heard from other perimenopausal women is *'I just don't know who I am any more.'* We can't easily do things we once took in our stride. We cry readily. We can't sleep. We're tired all the time. We forget what we're saying half-way through saying it. We feel angry for no reason. We feel like we're losing our minds.

Just as when we were adolescent girls, perimenopausal women have to contend with our bodies changing again: we don't look the same. Our bodies don't behave the same. We bleed too much or too little. We sweat copiously. Our faces break out more than they did when we were in Year Nine. We're hot all the time. We lay down fat in all the wrong places and it proves impossible to shift. And why the heck am I growing a beard?! I'm beginning to think that perimenopause isn't so much a borderland as a wasteland. A wasteland that's as hot and dry as Death Valley.

But if we first lost our sense of true self way back when, who even are we anyway? Sure, we grew up. We became functioning adults (or semi-functioning in my case) and we learned some self-control and how to better regulate our emotions. This was necessary to live a responsible adult life. We learned to temper our own egos and to consider other people. These are all markers of healthy adulthood; but feeling disconnected, disassociated and repressed are not, and these are all features of women's lives which can emerge during adolescence[7] and come out sideways during perimenopause.

Heartbreakingly, as the researchers followed the girls' journey from childhood through to their teen years, the words *'I don't know'* increasingly crept into their conversations. The girls are observed struggling over 'speaking and not speaking, knowing and not knowing, feeling and not feeling'.[8] That some of the girls are aware that this disconnection from themselves is happening is particularly painful. One girl refers to how her inner voice has been 'muffled'. She says, 'The voice that stands up for what I believe in has been buried deep inside of me.'[9] This is a comment that is indicative of what emerged over the course of the research from all the girls: disassociation. Disconnection. Repression.[10] This can't possibly be God's hope for girls and women.

What if some of the turbulence we experience during perimenopause is caused by our authentic self trying to claw her way out? Suppressed under layers of self-sacrifice, and attempts to live up to the impossible norms of church and culture, what if she's finally had enough and wants to break free? What if midlife is a time where we're invited to discover that the girl we thought was buried wasn't actually dead at all? What if she was only sleeping?

There is a story in the Synoptic Gospels which speaks into this situation powerfully and poignantly. It's the story of a girl restored to life and a woman healed, but it's more often known as the story of the woman with the menstrual bleeding issue, even though Mark, Matthew and Luke all tell it in tandem with the restoration of the girl, perhaps asking us to see these two stories as being in conversation with one another, and encouraging us to make links between the two.[11] The woman has been bleeding for twelve years and the girl is twelve years old, a time when the bleeding usually starts. Lutheran pastor Judith VanOsdol explains it thus:

> The two women are linked as sisters, bound by blood, marginalization and impending death. Together they represent both sides of the female condition: menarche and menopause.[12]

We encounter Jesus amid a crowd, being asked by Jairus, a local synagogue leader, to come and help his daughter, who is either lying at the point of death or has already died, depending which Gospel account we read. It's when Jesus is on his way to raise up the girl that he encounters the woman who is bleeding. The waking of the girl is *literally* interrupted by the bleeding woman. The detail of her persistent and heavy bleeding for twelve years is one that Elaine Storkey suggests puts her at the cusp of middle age,[13] a time we now know can herald the onset of perimenopause. Church of England priest Julie Gittoes has written about the story of the bleeding woman as being a useful way of talking about menopause. The stopping of the bleeding speaks of the transformation that takes place between perimenopause and 'the abating of blood at menopause'.[14] This is a story of a bleeding woman who draws near to Jesus in the hope he will heal her and in response Jesus brings about spontaneous menopause. She touches the fringe of his cloak and the bleeding stops.

Reimagining this story as being one of menopause is not to dismiss the pathology of this woman's bleeding. She could have been suffering from a number of possible issues including fibroids or endometriosis, a condition where uterine tissue grows in other parts of the body as well as the womb, causing debilitating pain and heavy bleeding. Sometimes there's no identifiable reason for heavy bleeding, and in this woman's case, we can only guess. Lots of women experience heavy and long spells of menstrual bleeding particularly during perimenopause, episodes that lead to us feeling drained, fatigued and anxious about our ability to carry on with our daily lives. It's something that's blighted my own life at various times, making me look forward to the day when the bleeding finally stops. For me, the bleeding woman is one of the most relatable characters in the Gospels.

This woman's life has been severely restricted by her bleeding body and her freedom curtailed. She lives in poverty after having been fobbed off and given the run around by physicians, who failed to provide her with any relief or a solution but took her money anyway. Her plight is usually told in the context of Jewish religious laws, where she's depicted as an outcast, prevented from participating in worship and community life due to her persistent bleeding. Leviticus 15.13–29 is the source for the public health laws that would have restricted her, as her abnormal bleeding rendered her permanently ritually impure, reflecting a concern with sickness rather than a distaste for menstrual bleeding, a concern that we might have more sympathy with now after having lived through the Covid-19 pandemic; in a time where disease was poorly understood, the laws prevented people from hanging out at the temple if they were unwell.[15] It's unclear whether her ritual impurity (which isn't mentioned in the text) would have even mattered in a local village so far away from the temple compound,[16] but it's still not hard for me to imagine how bleeding constantly might impact horribly on someone's life and how such a person might yearn for healing. That she desired to be made whole again by touching Jesus' cloak is the point of the story. She believed that his holiness would quite literally rub off on her.

Casting the treatment of this woman as a Levitical oddity distracts us from fully acknowledging that women and our bleeding bodies are still a deeply unpleasant taboo that lots of people would rather not discuss openly. To confront heavy bleeding and all its unpleasant side-effects, in a church no less, is still a hugely transgressive act. Women and our bleeding bodies can feel no more welcome today. The 'biological, fleshy and leaky presence of the woman priest',[17] for example, still feels like a direct challenge to the norm – the norm being male bodied, of course.

Outside the church, too, the physical experiences of women and the issues we might have with our bodies are routinely dismissed[18] and, just like the bleeding woman, feeling unheard by the medical profession when seeking help for gynaecological problems is a common concern.[19] This is exacerbated for those from marginalized groups. Black women, for example, are four times as likely as white women to die in pregnancy or childbirth,[20] a bias that continues into middle age where there is an inequality of perimenopause support offered to women from black, Asian and minority ethnic backgrounds.[21] The disregard for the experience of the bleeding woman is so much more than a throw-back to times long since gone; her life, just like the girls we learned about earlier, just like my life, and perhaps yours too, has been one of *disconnection, dissociation, repression.* 'Who touched me?' Jesus invites. When she opens her mouth and tells him the whole truth,[22] she speaks for us all.

The gears of the story of the bleeding woman shift when Jesus asks her to speak to him. The healing of this unheard woman is only complete when Jesus truly listens to her. She touches his cloak, is healed, and Jesus, sensing that the transformation has taken place, asks her to reveal herself. And note this: he insists she do this, not because he doesn't know who it was, but because he wants to listen to her story. He wants her to testify in front of the crowd, so everyone can hear, to what the marginalization of her bleeding body has done to her. Jesus doesn't shy away from her bleeding. He isn't revolted by her or embarrassed by her bodily functions. Her bleeding isn't taboo to him. Jesus invites us to see menopause not as a challenge to our faith but an opportunity to draw closer to him, tell him of our pain, and be renewed and strengthened.

But this is only half of the story, because when Jesus makes the bleeding stop, he immediately wakes up the girl. He goes at once to Jairus' house, a place that's noisy and chaotic with weeping and the sounds of hysterical mourning. He takes charge and clears everybody out who doesn't need to be there. 'Do not fear, only believe,' he says. Taking the girl's hand he speaks to her: *'Talitha Cum!'* (Girl, I say to you, arise!). Or, as we say in my house of a morning: 'WAKE UP!'

There are only a handful of Aramaic phrases in the Gospels, because despite this being the language that Jesus would have spoken, the Gospel writers chose to render their accounts into Greek. Why, then, does this phrase remain in its original form? Perhaps because the scene left such an impression on the listeners, this phrase ended up being repeated often when the story was told and retold.[23] It could also be that the Aramaic phrases were retained because they'd developed liturgical significance in the early worshipping communities.[24] I can't help but be moved that Jesus' command to this girl who is seemingly dead continues to be heard in the same words that she herself would have listened to in his own voice as he roused her from death.

When learning about the lives of girls for their study, *Meeting at the Crossroads*, Brown and Gilligan created what they called a 'Listener's Guide' which allowed them to explore the girls' development, by coming alongside them and listening deeply and attentively, not only to what the girls were saying, but also to *how* they were saying it. Their technique reminded me powerfully of Lectio Divina, a way of praying aloud through scripture using holy listening. It's a prayerful way of using the Bible to enter into what God might be trying to say to us. When you take the time to really listen, you tune into the frequency of the voices that usually can't be heard. Jesus listens to this woman and the girl inside the woman hears.

'Listening to girls, we began once again to know what we had come not to know.'[25] What did you once know but have since forgotten? Your body and soul recollect things you might not remember with your conscious mind. Your bones, your muscles, your innermost parts have memories that yearn to be told. You may have forgotten how to express those things but you didn't forget how to feel. There is knowing that happens at a cellular level and it can't be denied. I know this like I know the presence of God. Perimenopause is a crossroads I'm standing at right now. I expected to meet my mother and my grandmother there, and all the other women who have made this journey before me. I didn't expect to meet the girl I once was. I wonder, if I take her hand, what will she help me to remember?

She takes me to a memory of a beach in Gran Canaria. Crashing waves, high enough to be fun but not too high to wash people away. I'm wearing my knickers and nothing else, because this was an impromptu stop at the beach on the way back to the hotel after dinner, and I didn't have my swimming costume. No problem, I can just take off my t-shirt dress (picture of Minnie Mouse, white stretchy cotton, long fringes, *very* late '80s) and go in the sea in my undies. I'm nine years old and my body still belongs to me. I don't worry that my hair is tangled. I don't care that people might be watching me. I jump and splash with the kind of unbound abandon that only a nine-year-old child can experience, and the watching middle-aged me *began once again to know what I had come not to know*. That God did not create me to shrink and hide and feel anxious. That when Jesus said, *this is my body*, it was said for me too. That I am my body and my body is me. *Here she is*. Your body is you too. There is no separation between mind and flesh. Middle age is a time for us to see this as the heresy it is and to repent of it. We are our ageing, flawed, brilliant bodies. Aren't we marvellous? Menopause doesn't herald an abandonment of self. It's a time of reclamation.

One of the strangest things about getting older is that some parts of your soul refuse to play along. When the wrinkles arrived and the first grey hairs, and the world started seeing me as just another middle-aged mum, a portion of my soul chafed at this indifferent treatment. The world keeps trying to tell me I'm redundant, past it, expired, that I've exceeded my shelf-life, but the girl who still lives on didn't get the memo. She who exists as a tiny kernel deep inside me, curled up in foetal discomfort, squashed and smashed into a tiny space, too narrow and confined to let her stretch, test her true strength and breathe. How did I let that happen to her? That audacious girl who danced on the beach in her knickers, her flat chest salty with sea foam and her hair tangled and free. All that remains outwardly of her are the colony of freckles across my forehead and cheekbones, an artifact of being exposed to the sun at a time when parents played fast and loose with sun cream, and I, with my pale English skin, stood not a chance in hell of reaching adulthood unscathed.

What happened to her? Other than sunburn, of course. Like a time bomb destined to go off around the age of twelve, everything changed, nothing was fixed and her body didn't stay free. Its geography shifted from familiar flat plains to an unknown terrain that bulged and swelled and didn't belong to her any more. It was all rounded peaks and slopes and resisted her attempts to tame it, and suddenly, males who she encountered wanted to explore. It no longer belonged to her. Special equipment was required to make it behave and to contain it;

straps that dug into tender skin and wires that pinched. Thick pads made from cotton wool which bunched up into a useless sausage shape and failed to stem the flow (this was before the innovation of wings and a dry-weave top-sheet). Quinoderm for acne. Impulse to spray everywhere in order to hide the all new adult smells that this body seemed to permeate.

Eyes that dropped to her no longer bony chest. Boys who laughed when she ran because parts she'd rather keep hidden moved comically. She heard them laugh and felt bone-deep shame for this new body that had betrayed her. Almost as suddenly as the boys lost their ability to hit certain notes, she lost the full and free use of her emotional range. It was buried under a tyranny of being *nice* and *kind*.[26] The expression of certain feelings was no longer welcome. Anger was not lady-like. Being genuine was replaced with being polite. It was more important to be liked than to be real. To seek approval over authenticity. She learned how to speak without saying anything.

She became physically restricted. Blood on her school skirt. Days missed due to being doubled up with pain on the sofa, curled around a hot water bottle, bleeding copiously but with no regularity. It appeared on day trips to theme parks. It appeared during PE. It appeared when she wanted to wear tight white jeans or a swimming costume. It was a painful inconvenience. Her body felt like it was no longer her. At some point a fracture occurred between body and soul, and this damaged her in ways she couldn't even recognize. She didn't know about God back then. She didn't realize that she was fearfully and wonderfully made. As she got older she met a few snakes. She ate so much bad fruit it made her sick. And eventually, she forgot all about the girl she once was.

Until now.

I believe in the power of Jesus to restore. I believe that he can make all things new. I pray that menopausal women will experience new adventures. I pray and hope that Jesus can raise us to new life. He will wake us up, and our freedom to be who he made us will be restored, unencumbered by the things that may have held us back. Jesus is going to burst in and shout at everyone to clear out, because he's got work to do. He's going to make us come alive. He's going to boldly declare so that everyone can hear, 'Girl, I say to you, arise!' And then we'll take her hand and dance on the beach and give zero damns who sees us do it.

Notes

1 *The Message* translation.

2 Bridges Johns, C., *Seven Transforming Gifts of Menopause: An unexpected spiritual journey* (Grand Rapids: Brazos Press, 2020).

3 Brown, L. Mikel and Gilligan, C., *Meeting at the Crossroads: Women's psychology and girls' development* (Cambridge: Harvard University Press, 1992, p. 36).

4 Brown and Gilligan, *Meeting at the Crossroads*.

5 Gittoes, J., 'Her bleeding stopped: The embodied borderland of the menopause', http://juliegittoes.blogspot.com/2021/10/her-bleeding-stopped-embodied.html (accessed 27.4.24).

6 Brown and Gilligan, *Meeting at the Crossroads* (p. 22).

7 Brown and Gilligan, *Meeting at the Crossroads* (p. 76).

8 Brown and Gilligan, *Meeting at the Crossroads* (p. 28).

9 Brown and Gilligan, *Meeting at the Crossroads* (p. 104).

10 Brown and Gilligan, *Meeting at the Crossroads* (p. 28).

11 Mark 5.21–43; Matthew 9.18–26; Luke 8.40–56.

12 VanOsdol, J., 'Talitha Cum: The raising up of women and girls to overcome violence', Overcoming Violence: Churches Seeking Reconciliation and Peace (World Council of Churches, 2011), http://www.overcomingviolence.org/en/resources-dov/wcc-resources/documents/bible-studies/talitha-cum-the-raising-up-of-women-and-girls-to-overcome-violence.html (accessed 26.4.24).

13 Storkey, E., 'The Bleeding Woman', *Woman Alive*, 9 May 2019, https://www.elainestorkey.com/woman-alive-series/ (accessed 26.4.24).

14 Gittoes, 'Her bleeding stopped'.

15 Young-Somers, D., 'It Says what?!', Zoom conversation hosted by JW3 London, https://www.youtube.com/watch?v=mToldJ8hQ7M&t=263s (accessed 26.4.24).

16 Levine, A.-J. and Zvi Brettler, M. (eds), *The Jewish Annotated New Testament, New Revised Standard Bible Translation* (Oxford: Oxford University Press, 2011).

17 Jagger, S., 'Presiding like a Woman: Menstruating at the Altar', in Cocksworth, A., Starr, R. and Burns, S. (eds) with Nicola Slee, *From the Shores of Silence: Conversations in Feminist Practical Theology* (London: SCM Press, 2023, p. 144).

18 A recent study found that women were more likely than men to have their pain dismissed and underestimated, in Lang, Z., Reynolds Losin, E., Asher, Y., Koban, L. and Wager, T., 'Gender Biases in Estimation of Others' Pain', *Journal of Pain*, 22(9), September 2021, https://www. jpain.org/article/S1526-5900(21)00035-3/fulltext (accessed 26.4.24).

19 Dervish-O'Kane, R., 'Gender Health Gap: 8 in 10 UK Women Report Not Being Listened to by Healthcare Professionals', *Women's Health*, 23 December 2021, https://www.womenshealthmag.com/uk/ health/female-health/a38599769/gender-health-gap/ (accessed 26.4.24).

20 Summers, H., 'Black women in the UK four times more likely to die in pregnancy or childbirth', *The Guardian*, 15 January 2021, https:// www.theguardian.com/global-development/2021/jan/15/black-women- in-the-uk-four-times-more-likely-to-die-in-pregnancy-or-childbirth (accessed 26.4.24).

21 'Every menopause matters' (*The Hippocratic Post*, 28 June 2023), https://www.hippocraticpost.com/womens-health/every-menopause- matters/#:~:text=Every%20menopause%20matters%3A%20New %20research,the%20experience%20of%20white%20women (accessed 26.4.24).

22 Mark 5.34.

23 Wright, T., *Mark for Everyone* (London: SPCK, 2001).

24 VanOsdol, 'Talitha Cum'.

25 Brown and Gilligan, *Meeting at the Crossroads* (p. 29).

26 Brown and Gilligan, *Meeting at the Crossroads* (p. 133).

We set out on the second day

The things we leave behind

As the sun rises in the sky, we lace up our boots, don our rucksacks, and set off on our second day in the wilderness. We've packed our tents up, folding the canvas into tightly packed wads, as small and as compact as we possibly can. Our enamel mugs and aluminium cooking gear dangles from our bags, jingling noisily, puncturing the still air with a sound that doesn't belong to this land. We don't belong to the wilderness either, but we must somehow make our way here.

We've helped one another to pack as lightly as possible, but some baggage can't be managed alone. There are those of us who carry too much, and as we hike over hill and rock, with the rising sun growing ever hotter, the burden quickly becomes unmanageable. We must stop and take stock of the things we've brought along on the journey and ask ourselves if there are things we really need to be carrying. Are there heavy things we can take off our backs and leave behind?

There were burdens we brought with us into the wilderness, stuff that we thought was essential for our survival, but as we trek further into the unknown we realize that the things we thought we needed aren't so important after all. We're starting to realize the things we've taken for granted might turn out to be what we're left holding when all is said and done.

We take the weight off our shoulders and in a moment of energetic defiance, we throw everything on the ground. The girl who came along with us laughs with joy at our antics. She brought barely anything with her at all and yet she still seems to have everything she needs. Her laughter is as light as the burdens she carries in her miniature rucksack.

In the emptying we discover we've been carrying things we'd forgotten we'd packed; things that were squashed and crumpled up into the deepest recesses of our bags but were deceptively heavy. We've been carrying them around for too long and they're holding us back. Old things. Stale things. Useless things. Broken things. Things that served us once but lost their purpose long ago. Things we never really needed but which we hung onto because we were scared to let go. Some things we've carried for years and we've long since forgotten the reasons why. Things we've always used out of habit and without thinking. Things that no longer fit. Things we don't even recognize.

Onto the ground they go, to join the pile of other detritus and rubbish from the first half of our lives. So much of it is useless to us now. Why on earth have we been carrying it all for so long? Without all the stuff we don't need, we must rely on diminished resources, but that's OK. Now we have the clarity to see what's necessary, instead of always having to root around to seek out what's essential amid the clutter. We have everything we need.

This day we will tread a little more confidently. We will hold our heads a little bit higher. We will laugh more readily. Unencumbered by the weight of the burdens that have held us back, we will stand a little straighter. Our hearts already feel lighter. The girl smiles with encouragement.

Onwards we go.

3

The freedom to lose

An emphasis on recreating an area's
natural, uncultivated state.
The Woodland Trust describing rewilding

I'm increasingly concerned there's a rewilding project happening on my face. As an ordained deacon I know I'm called to be a Christlike presence in the world, but I didn't know this would involve growing to *actually look* like Christ, complete with beard and increasingly unkempt hair. And not Jim Caviezel Jesus either, but the far less sexy 1970s Robert Powell era Jesus. I'd prefer that my *Jesus-y* qualities were restricted to the desire to exchange water for wine and reserving the right to lose it every now and again by claiming, '*I'm just turning tables over, dammit!*' But perhaps Christian discipleship is like the film *The Santa Clause*, where Tim Allen gradually transforms into an old guy with a bearded face and bloated paunch, after unwittingly entering into a contract to become the next Santa. Maybe the holier I am, the hairier my face will become and the more open-toed and uglier will be my taste in footwear. Either way, middle age means that my tweezers are now my top item to have with me if stranded on a desert island.

Rewilding Britain, a charity dedicated to returning ecosystems to their natural state as a solution to the climate crisis, sees rewilding as a paradigm for hope. Its goals are restoring what once was, reinstating the natural order of things, and recovering what was lost. Research has shown that bringing things back to life leads to healing and recovery. Who knew that a wilderness could do all that! Well, Jesus did. He deliberately put himself in the danger of the wilderness, outside the comfortable and safe confines of all he knew, eschewing power and control, welcoming discomfort, just so he could prove it could be done. It was the wilderness that prepared him for what was to come, for the mission that was his alone. Because when you're in a wild place that you don't recognize, where the familiar things you normally depend on count for nothing, you're forced to turn inwards to rely on whatever inner resources you still carry. The person who emerges after a prolonged stint in the wilderness is not the same one who went in.

The wilderness of menopause has always been a social frontier for women, long before humans acquired the language and the terminology to describe it.[1] It may well be a time of trial, of profound discomfort, confusion or even suffering, but this doesn't mean it's not fruitful. It's a necessary transition and in my experience transitions usually hurt like hell but are worth it in the end. A transition begins with an ending and finishes with a beginning,[2] a profoundly Christian concept. My faith is in a God who died so that we could begin again, a resurrection that no one saw coming when they were in the grief and wilderness of Holy Saturday. The God who is the Alpha and the Omega knows all about the power of transition.

It's also a term used in midwifery to describe the indescribable; that moment when a woman is so overwhelmed by the intensity and power of the contractions that she despairs and feels she can't go on. This is usually a sign that she's ready to push and is transitioning from stage one of labour to stage two; the birthing pains will soon be over and new life will begin. I've birthed four babies and I remember this moment very well; the contractions come so fast they are on top of one another, giving you no space to pause and catch your breath between them. If you've managed without pain relief up to this point, this is the moment where you might lose control and suddenly start begging for an epidural (which you won't be allowed to have at this stage, by the way). You feel like you're going to break in two and be utterly destroyed because nobody can hope to survive this agony. The pain has no beginning and no ending. You exist inside the pain and there is nothing else in the universe except it and you. It feels like it will never end, which floors you by a despair so powerful you're certain you can't go on any more. And then, *just like that*, the urge to push arrives in an overwhelming tidal wave of pressure, and in the hard work of bearing down, the pain becomes a secondary force to the one compelling your body to squeeze birth into being. The pressure-pain means new life is about to begin.

Transition. It's a slow process involving losses and gains. I lost so much of myself when I became a mother; I lost my life as I'd known it but I gained the privilege of shaping someone else's. It's been a journey of suffering and happiness, of grief and joy, of many tiny deaths along the way, and just as many resurrections. I know that midlife and menopause will also involve this kind of holy exchange, because that's how God works.

Jesus said: 'Those who find their life will lose it, and those who lose their life for my sake will find it' (Matthew 10.39). A promise repeated (to varying degrees) in Matthew 16.25; Mark 8.35; Luke 9.24; Luke 17.33; and John 12.25. Jesus is talking specifically about the things we must die to in order to live a life in the fullness of God. There is a timeless truth to be found in knowing that nothing of real worth or value is achieved without sacrifice. There is no gain without some kind of loss.

I'd love to bring you tidings of gladness and joy (and I promise I will, in due course) but as your sister in Christ I must tell you that midlife and menopause is an endless, soul-sucking series of losses and gains. You will gain, for example, a face full of fuzz, but you will gradually lose your eyesight, so you won't notice it as much. You will gain, almost overnight, at least ten pounds just by looking at one tangy cheese Dorito, but you will lose the ability to stay awake after one glass of wine, thus negating you quaffing the entire bottle. You will lose your youthful glow but you will gain a face as red as a baboon's rear end and the ability to sweat copiously at random intervals. You will lose the capacity to sleep through the night but you'll gain the ability to fall asleep on the sofa before 9 p.m. every evening. You will lose your memory and not be able to recall your second child's name, but you'll gain full recall of every embarrassing, mortifying thing you ever did twenty-five years ago, and your brain will treat you to a little gag-reel every night, usually at 2 a.m. See? You lose some and then ... you lose some more.

We may have to woman-up and face facts: if menopause is a wilderness, then tired props aren't going to get us very far. The behaviours and habits we fell back on to survive womanhood in a world set up to cater mainly to male preferences won't help us to survive in a wilderness set up to cater to no one. If you've somehow managed to thrive in a world that praised you for your external *gifts*, you're going to have to start cultivating other gardens instead. Beauty is a contest for the young, and midlife is a time when we can gladly, and with some relief, retire from the arena, or make ourselves miserable by still desperately trying to compete. This is a realization that probably came earlier to you if you never measured up to narrow beauty norms because you were *too this*, or *too much that*, or conversely, never, ever enough; let's be honest, that's most of us! The wilderness is the place where the rug gets pulled from underneath the so-called lucky ones who did measure up, and now's the time for us all to see the truth: the rug was just an illusion anyway. Let's burn the thing and use it to keep warm.

Cheryl Bridges Johns writes:

As you watch your body age, you may be tempted to believe the best years of your life are in the past. They are not. Menopause is not the bearer of death; it signals the arrival of renewed time.[3]

When I was younger I had so much time to use up; years and years stretching ahead of me, and at the same time, I wasted life like it was single-use plastic. Disposable. Meaningless. A bounty that was squandered. Age has taught me that life is scarce and abundantly precious. It's not to be wasted and frittered away.

Having picked up and carried many crosses for Jesus and, at the risk of appearing mercenary, I'm interested in what he has to say about what we gain in return. What is the nature of this Jesus-life that he promises us? Losing your life to find it is linked to Jesus' promise that we have life abundantly. Not just eternal life, as this sells the Christian way so short. In truth, I rarely think of life after death. Despite what some atheists claim, I didn't become a Christian just so I'd have something to take away the sting of death. I'm far more interested in the here and now, and what these passages have to say about how we live out our life of faith, day to day.

Jesus' comment about abundant life comes from a story in John 10. The full verse goes like this:

'The thief comes only to steal and kill and destroy. I came that they may have life, and have it abundantly.' (John 10.10)

This is part of a parable about sheep, the gate and the good shepherd. Jesus uses different images for himself to describe his relationship to the sheep, to us. He's the gate by which the sheep enter the safety of the sheepfold; the sheep listen to his voice and are protected – saved – by him. Unlike thieves, who steal and maim, Jesus offers abundant life. In Paula Gooder's translation, the word abundant is swopped out for *extraordinarily*: 'I come so that they might have life and they might have it extraordinarily.'[4] This may well be one of the most luscious promises Jesus gives us. Who wouldn't want *life extraordinarily*? The Greek word being translated is *perissos*, which can have a wide range of meanings, including abundant, but we could also accurately use remarkable. It's a word that refers to quantity as well as quality;[5] Jesus is promising us a remarkable, extraordinary life and tons of it. That's quite the boast. It might even be worth dying to self for.

I've encountered many thieves throughout my life, people and situations that robbed me of my self-esteem, my confidence, my peace and contentment, and in some cases, warped my identity as a bearer of God's image. Navigating early womanhood in a world that continues to objectify female bodies and treat women as lesser humans, robbed me of the fullness of who God created me to be. Thieves of sexism and abuse left me shrunken and inflicted hairline fractures on my soul that I'm only now starting to fully repair. Jesus may well be the gate, the one we pass through to access the abundant life he promises us, but I weary of remaining in the safety of the sheepfold. I want to stretch my legs and enjoy the freedom and liberty of a life lived fully.

Amid the wildness of this midlife passage through the wastes of menopause, I'm finally ready to embrace Jesus' promise of abundant life; so much life you don't know what to do with it. Life that overflows and spills out everywhere like a freshly baked loaf, bursting out of its tin, or a curvy woman in a skin-tight dress. Life so abundant that it wants to break free and refuses to be confined. Resplendent life. Uncontainable life. Sensual, seeping, voluminous life. I want to recapture the me who danced on that beach and live again a time that was positively oozing with life. Life seeping out of the experience and running onto the ground; life between my toes and splashed onto my skin. Life caught in my hair and sucked into my lungs. Glorious life. If you've reached middle age, I'm hoping you have many examples of a life well lived. Maybe you've done incredible things and been to amazing places, but I wish someone had told the young me that the little moments were what it was all going to be about. I spent so much time either not noticing them or always reaching for something grander. I wish I'd known that it wasn't about the big moments born out of planning and expense. This promise for life abundant comes from Jesus, so the moments will be humble, like him. Emmanuel, who deliberately eschewed the high life and the status and privilege that would have gone along with it. The God who was born in a barn wants to show us that life extraordinarily does not mean an all-inclusive, access all areas, first-class, VIP pass to the good life. It doesn't mean those exclusive moments. This is life that's available for us all, not just those who can afford it.

My youngest child squeezing his bony arms around my neck and whispering that he loves me. Cuddled up in bed with my husband, listening to the rain fall on our roof. Chocolate melting on my tongue after forty days of Lent. A curry hot enough to make my eyes water. Unexpectedly hearing a song I danced to when I was eighteen and feeling my heart soar. Scarlet lipstick. Coffee and cake with my mum. Making my kids laugh. The feel of my dog's fur under my fingertips. The first roses unfurling on the bush I planted. The smell of the air on a frosty day in early spring. The sound of the ocean. The God-joy of Christian worship. Shimmering heat rising from the paschal candle. Curls of incense whispering in the dry and smoky air. The organ pipes shuddering with the opening bars of 'O Come, O Come, Emmanuel' on Advent Sunday. Shaking the dear bones of a paper-thin, sinewy hand and uttering 'Peace be with you'. Bread on my tongue. Sweet wine in my throat. Unto the ages of ages. World without end. Life extraordinarily.

Midlife and menopause are the gifts God gives us so we can enjoy life more abundantly, because we are given the wisdom to know life's worth. Even if while going through it you might be tempted to think it's a really rubbish gift, like the time my brother bought me an iron for Christmas. An unexciting, utilitarian, downright offensive offering, which none the less helped me straighten everything out. It's about having the clarity to see the giftedness in the things we find hard and recognizing the moments of grace and wonder that hide in the plain sight of ordinariness.

One of my daughter's favourite childhood films was *Inside Out*, a Disney animation about a twelve-year-old girl called Riley. Most of the action takes place inside Riley's head where we meet her personified emotions: Disgust, Fear, Anger, Joy and Sadness. These emotions all work together to help Riley navigate her new life in the city her parents have just moved the family to, but like many tweenagers in this position, Riley struggles to settle in. She misses her old life, her friends, her hockey team, and the sadder she feels, the more the Joy character tries to exert herself in order to fix it. Joy wants to dominate the other emotions, crowding out and silencing Sadness, so that Riley doesn't have to experience an emotion that Joy has decided is unwelcome. Riley learns that she must pretend to be happy when she's not, lest she disappoint her parents, who are desperate for her to settle in. Riley tries hard to conform to their image of her; happy equals good and nice. Sad equals bad and ungrateful. The end result of holding it all in is catastrophic confusion; everything gradually breaks down, family bonds and relationships, trust, security. Without the ability to access the full range of her emotions, Riley discovers that she can't feel anything at all. Anyone who has experienced deep depression will know how terrifying this void can be, the blank nothingness of an emotional vacuum. No ups, no downs, just an empty flatline of feeling. To heal Riley, Joy realizes that Sadness is the missing part of the puzzle. In order to feel right again, Riley needs to be free to express sadness.

The most profound lesson of my midlife journey so far has been acknowledging that sorrow shares a border with joy, and it's this truth that characterizes my faith. I think I always knew this, but it was one of the facets of my God-given nature that was supressed under the pressure to always appear nice. As a girl, I learned that to not smile when told to wasn't polite. My refusal to play this game has mostly been met with opposition. The world values women who grin and bear it far more than it does those who refuse to pretend. To quote one of our lesser-known saints, St Dolly of Parton: 'Laughter through tears is my favourite emotion.'[6] This is the true story of the church. Joy blended with sorrow. One doesn't work without the other.

The church so often dishonours this truth by refusing to acknowledge that sadness is part of the fabric of our faith. 'Come in!' Joy loudly proclaims. 'Nothing but positivity to see here!' When in reality, Sadness has been locked in a cupboard in the vestry and isn't allowed to join in with the worship. (Anger is shut in there too and is absolutely steaming about it; more on this in Chapter 4.) It's jarring if you're experiencing the full force of menopausal upheaval with all its attendant miseries when it collides with the brick wall of toxic positivity. We can end up asking ourselves if our pain is even welcome. Is our discomfort allowed? Is menopause welcome in the church at all? A church that's unable to stand up and honestly claim and name those things that have sinfully been labelled distasteful is not a place that feels nourishing for the faith of midlife women.

Christians are often fearful of sharing a faith that isn't shiny and attractive to look at because we're concerned people won't come along with us if we're honest about what's hidden behind the curtain. We've forgotten that so many of the people we want to welcome into our churches don't just need a place to experience joy, they need somewhere to freely share their sadness. We don't always need to make a joyful noise; sometimes the most honest thing the church can do is howl with sorrow and welcome the mournful to howl along with us.

The liturgical year (another way of describing the church calendar) gives us plenty of space to acknowledge the sorrow along with the joy. The rhythm built into it of fast and feast, lament and celebration, waiting and doing, song and silence, all of it is designed to facilitate the coming together of the human story with the story of God. Too much of one element puts the whole thing out of balance. It can't always be summertime. We can't always lie fallow. One must merge into the other. Rising and falling. Death and resurrection. The summer of youth, shifting slowly like a setting sun into the autumn of midlife. The hard graft to bring in the harvest, followed by the abundant sweetness of the fruit. Maybe by the time middle age comes around, you're finally ripe, but in order for the harvest gifts to be brought in, the sharp bite of the sickle needs to come in first.

Your menopause experience will likely contain sorrow, but I pray you will also experience joy. Sometimes you may have to seek it out in unexpected places, but then there it will be, like a speck of glitter briefly dazzling your eye. Tiny and fleeting, but all the more precious because of it. It probably won't look how you expect it to look, this God-joy, this *life extraordinarily*. Like the cup of Christ and the man who held it to his lips, it will be humble and hardly worth the noticing to anyone who hasn't the time to pause and look. Amanda Held Opelt wrote in *Holy Unhappiness*:

> In a culture that says, 'more is more', the great protest of the Christian is to say, 'enough is enough'.[7]

If sorrow and joy share a border, together they make a place called contentment, and I can't say 'Amen' enough to that.

Let me tell you the best part of my day. My husband walks into our bedroom every morning and places a mug of coffee on my bedside table. The smell of the coffee heralds his arrival as it escapes the kitchen and permeates the house, whispering up the stairs. He comes in with this fragrant offering, wearing his plush dressing gown, his silver-black hair mussed and his eyes bruised from sleep, and he gives me a smile that's so sweet it pinches my heart. Every day this happens, without fail. Every day he gets up first. Every day the kettle goes on. I hear it whistling and then moments later smell the roasted beans soaking in the boiled water. Every day he loves me, without exception. It is the best part of my day. This is what Jesus meant by life abundant, I'm sure. And if that wasn't what he meant by abundant life, then I don't want it, because that moment right there, that's perfection. Enough is more than enough.

Lose your life and find it.

Lose your way but find other paths to follow.

Lose your mind but find yourself trusting in your senses.

Lose your youth but find wisdom.

Lose your concentration but find new ways of knowing.

Lose your fertility but find that creating new life is still possible in so many other ways.

Lose your beauty but find you have value more profound and wonderful than that which is skin-deep.

Lose your status in the eyes of the world but find a greater purpose through the lens of God.

Lose yourself utterly but find what once was gone. Renewed. Remade. Reforged. Finally free. Thank you, Jesus.

Notes

1 Mattern, S., *The Slow Moon Climbs: The Science, History and Meaning of Menopause* (Princeton: Princeton University Press, 2019).

2 Bridges, W., *Managing Transitions: Making the Most of Change* (London: Nicholas Brealey Publishing, 2017, p. 21).

3 Bridges Johns, C., *Seven Transforming Gifts of Menopause* (Grand Rapids: Brazos Press, 2020, p. 121).

4 Gooder, P., *The Parables* (London: Canterbury Press, 2020, p. 57).

5 Gooder, *The Parables*.

6 This is actually a line from the character played by Dolly in the film *Steel Magnolias*, but she says it so beautifully that I'm claiming it as a Dollyism.

7 Held Opelt, A., *Holy Unhappiness: God, Goodness and the Myth of the Blessed Life* (New York: Hachette Book Group, 2023).

We fall out on the third day

Flipping off the wilderness

Why did we think this would be an easy journey, with clear paths and obvious trails to follow? Today we've learned that it's not; an obvious way forward sometimes hides from us underneath overgrown shrubs and bushes, forcing us to hack our way through with whatever makeshift tools we can pick up along the way. Our arms and legs get scratched, and we pick up bits of debris in our hair and our clothing gets torn, proof that we fought our way through and didn't come out the other end unscathed. The sun burns down hotly. We sweat under our sunhats and caps. Tempers become frayed. We bicker about which is the right way to go; some say the recognizable trail to the right, some say we pick our way carefully along the rockier, more perilous path to the left, and some, the girl among them, favour the way straight ahead. There is no clear path at all, only undergrowth and scrub, an impassable hellscape of sharp prickles and trailing creepers. A way to trip and fall. A way to be cut and grazed. A way to get lost in and maybe never come out.

'Let's go this way,' the girl implores. 'It'll be fun!'

Someone mumbles, 'I told you we shouldn't have brought her along.'

We argue about what to do next, and the group threatens to split into three. The younger women want the easier path; they're tired and they want out of this wilderness as quickly as possible. They've got things to do and people to see on the other side. There are those of us who want to walk the middling option of the rocky path; we know that the journey will have challenges and we're willing to meet them, just not *too many* challenges. Besides which, the rocky path follows the coast and we might have a lovely view of the ocean if we go that way.

The oldest among us try to smooth things over; they've been here before. They agree with the girl that the way straight ahead is where we must go. Even though it seems to be impossible to navigate, and even though it will make our journey harder and longer, they recall that this was the way they travelled when they came through the wilderness. It looks all wrong, but it's the right way to go.

We can't agree. The younger women are reluctant to listen to the wisdom of their older sisters; they have their own priorities according to their own place in time and an upbringing informed by a culture very different to that which their older sisters were raised in. They think that the older women don't care how they feel. The older women feel unappreciated and unheard. Nobody feels understood. It seems to be an unbreachable gap and the width of it threatens to prevent these women learning from each other. Underneath it all lies an unpalatable truth that no one wants to address; the women are old and this is something that younger women have been taught to fear. They see the faces of their older sisters; the lines, the grey hairs, the thoughts and opinions that were born out of a different age, the scorn and indifference with which older women are treated by the world, and they fear this happening to them. They feel alienated from one another. But the younger women must make this journey too, and it can't be completed unless they learn from those who went before.

Voices are raised, unrested mouths say foolish things that will be regretted afterwards, emotions bubble over or inwardly seethe, and we still can't agree. In the end, it is the girl who decides.

She suddenly throws her head back, opens her mouth and screams. The sound echoes over the valleys, tumbling through the canyons, scattering birds and sending them flying into the air. An unseen animal screams back in response.

The women stop arguing abruptly, their own mouths gaping

wide in alarm and surprise. One mouth starts to twitch. Then another. And another. A tsunami of laughter breaks over the group, gaining in volume and mirth as the women are each overcome with the ridiculousness of the situation, with the absurdity of it all. Mumbled words of apology issue forth. Hugs are asked for and given. Tears of relief are hastily wiped away.

'Feel better now?' the girl asks.

'Yes,' we say, exhausted but oddly jubilant.

'Good,' she grins. 'It's better if you don't hold it in. Can we go now?'

We shrug our bags onto our backs, younger women helping the older ones to their feet. A smooth hand squeezes a weathered one. Eyes encircled by wrinkles crinkle knowingly and the clear and unlined ones wink in reply.

We march onwards, walking straight ahead together.

4

Inviting Anger to pull up a pew

'Do not be fooled, there is no gentleness in me.'
The Kelham Madonna[1]

Anger stirs, awake once again. At midlife, Anger rarely sleeps. The combination of dwindling hormones and decades of frustration won't allow her to rest. She simmers in the background, suppressed and pushed down, unwelcome and unwanted like the bad fairy uninvited to the christening feast. But Lifetide turns and those things which have been hidden shall be secreted no more. Now it's harvest time for Anger. It's her moment to shine. Anger buckles the sequin belt of truth about her waist and she slips the high heels of righteousness upon her feet. She grabs the leather handbag of faith and upon her head she places the leopard print beret of salvation. Clothed in justice, Anger steps out of the closet. She towers over Niceness, who quails at the sight of her. Anger is quite a thing to behold. She points a finger in the face of Niceness and she says, 'Not today, Satan.' Anger says enough is enough. She refuses to pipe down. She calls a spade a spade. She says, *'This isn't fair.'* She's unafraid to declare, *'This is wrong.'* Anger has had enough. Anger shouts, *'No more!'* Anger refuses to be contained and she demands to stand in line and take her place beside Joy and Sadness and all the others. I am one of you, she says. I belong here too. And I will not be silenced.

Within every Christian woman lives the message: 'An angry woman is evil and sinful' or 'An angry woman is a bitch'.[2] This is massively inconvenient because the feeling that is expressed most often among menopausal women I've spoken to is anger. Menopausal women can feel inexplicable and searing rage, often for seemingly no reason at all. This anger manifests itself by irritation at loved ones, a sense of injustice that things aren't as they're supposed to be, or just a pervasive feeling of being pissed off at the planet, at the church, at God, at ourselves.

In a world which remains uncomfortable with women's anger, while inciting and tolerating the baser instincts of men, the church remains a place where passionate feelings are frowned upon and where niceness is promulgated as a feminine virtue. Angry? Be nice. Frustrated? Be nice. Resentful? Be nice. Choking on hormonal rage so colossal you could uproot an oak tree? Swallow it down, suppress it, take the impact internally so it ricochets inside you like exploding shrapnel, but whatever you do *be nice.*

Once again, I find myself leafing through my Bible, fruitlessly searching for the passage in the Gospels where Jesus says, *'Just be nice, OK?'* Nope. Can't find it. What I do find is Jesus lashing out at Peter in frustration, calling people robbers and thieves and threatening them with a corded whip, telling his mother and family hard and unpalatable truths, and implying a woman is a dog. Whatever else Jesus was, he categorically was not nice.

A church which promotes niceness as a virtue and refuses to admit to or allow its members to express, albeit in safe and boundaried ways, the full spectrum of human emotion is one which denies that Christians are fully human. And if we deny our own humanity, how can we ever have redemptive, beautiful things to tell the world about the humanity of God? The wonder of the incarnation is a hollow mystery if we ourselves are unable to articulate by our actions and our worship that we even comprehend what is meant by fully human.

So much of our behaviour as Christians is formed by the good intention of wanting to live out our calling as disciples faithfully, but getting to grips with grace is hard. You can't make God love you more just by being nicer. God knows your thoughts and your heart and is intimately acquainted with your anger. God's aware that you secretly yearn to give that annoying person playing thrash metal full blast on the train a roundhouse kick to the head, despite you enduring this indignity nicely with Christian fortitude. Those feelings aren't going anywhere, no matter how you try to hide them. (God, the victorious warrior, would surely exalt with you if you took affirmative action, as would everyone else in the train carriage. Have at it, Christian soldier.)

Women are particularly prone to this repudiation of our true nature because we haven't been permitted to express so-called negative emotions in healthy ways, and because we've learned through bitter experience that giving full reign to our emotions comes with consequences. Instead of the church supporting and encouraging us to do this, what we end up with is the pandemic of passive aggression that characterizes so much of public Christian discourse, particularly on social media, and is also present in our interpersonal interactions. Both men and women can be guilty of passive aggression, but in my experience, it is women who have made it into an artform. Give me a rude and boorish man being insufferable to my face any day of the week over a woman sniping behind my back with her friends, then greeting me with fake smiles. Neither is welcome, but at least the first option can be tackled head-on, whereas the passive-aggressive response is impossible to challenge. The person engaging in this insidious behaviour always has the fallback of plausible deniability, because it's characterized by covert, implied actions, tone and body language, making being on the receiving end of it isolating and hugely disempowering.

Returning briefly to *Meeting at the Crossroads* and the research done with young girls, one of the features of development identified over the course of the study was that girls were encouraged to self-sacrifice and self-silence in order to attain goals of purity and perfection, because they'd taken on the messaging that these were conditions for relationship and were the mark of a good woman.[3] This is in sharp contrast to the subliminal and overt messaging that boys receive, such as dominance and self-aggrandizement promoted as desirable qualities. In a similar study undertaken by clinical psychologist Annie Rogers, she studied the concept of ordinary courage by exploring the etymology of the word: *'To speak one's mind by telling all one's heart.'* She observed that girls between ages of eight and twelve gradually lost their ordinary courage as they grew up and hit adolescence, conforming to external expectations which led them to forfeit their voice, resilience and self-confidence.[4]

Engaging in passive-aggressive behaviour as a way to deal with conflict or unpleasant emotions is one way this might manifest in adult life, and this surely goes double for the church; if anger is censured then letting it escape in surreptitious ways, under the radar, is an inevitable consequence.

I was shocked when, at age thirty-three, I joined the church to discover that Christians aren't above acting like this. I had naively assumed that knowing Jesus would prompt people to behave better; that communication would be open, honest and healthy. Instead, I encountered envy, petty resentments, ambition, competitiveness and, on occasion, pure spite. Underneath all this negativity festered anger, like asbestos hidden away in the cavities of the walls, every poisonous interaction knocked plaster off and unleashed more fragments of noxious dust, choking the life out of that particular church. Nothing was acknowledged and nothing was ever dealt with, and so it worsened, causing unimaginable harm. I took from this experience one unassailable truth that I've never forgotten: a church without conflict is not a church without conflict. It's just a church where conflict is never permitted.

I was raised in an atheist environment amid a family of mouthy extroverts, emoting and tossing out opinions endlessly. It was exhausting but it taught me never to bottle anything up, and that I could argue freely with people and speak my mind, because I would still be loved afterwards. It taught me that anger isn't the end of the world. I wish I could say the same about the church, but I can't. Since becoming a Christian, and especially since hitting middle age, I've felt that my true self is unwelcome in the church; that I must hide and veil my feelings because they aren't wanted. And the feeling that's top of the list of the unwelcome is anger.

A healthy theology of anger should include space for people to acknowledge without shame that they experience angry thoughts and that there's no sin in feeling that way. John Wesley might have thought that when humans were sanctified, they would no longer experience anger, but he also wrote: 'Anger at sin we allow.'[5] And Martin Luther, a man not known for his mild manners and temperate nature, wrote:

If I want to write, pray, preach well, then I must be angry.
Then my entire blood supply refreshes itself, my mind is made
keen, and all temptations depart.[6]

Anger is part of us, whether we like it or not, and it may well
be a large feature of our menopausal journey. If our image of
God is one of a kindly, benevolent being, with the angry God
who thunders with wrath and vengeance relegated to the Old
Testament, replaced by gentle Jesus (an anti-Semitic idea, for the
record), then who in heaven do we turn to when we ourselves
desire vengeance? I'm going to go out on a limb and assume that
you're as human as I am, and therefore you're also susceptible
to the ungraciousness and meanness of spirit that I fall prey
to. It can't just be me who wants to stab out some well-chosen
words to school the arrogant asshat/brother in Christ, who is
well actually-ing me for all it's worth in the comments section.
I can't be the only person who yearns to flip off the Audi driver
who is viciously tailgating me on the M6. I can't be the only
person who still nurtures an irrational and bone-deep hatred
for Jar Jar Binks. (OK, that might well be just me, but hope-
fully you take the point.) If your God isn't spacious enough to
accommodate wrath, vengeance and hate, and only ever makes
room for polite niceties and noxious cheeriness, then that's not
God. That's a children's TV presenter.

Some things in this world are worthy of our rage, indeed
sometimes, anger is the only acceptable emotion. I believe in
a God who is as outraged by injustice as I am. Who is incan-
descent with rage at the horrors people inflict on one another. A
God who is moved to attacks of white-hot fury as well as bouts
of boundless, soothing love. Naming and claiming our darkest
emotions, however unpleasant the church might find them, is a
prophetic chore that we must undertake for the sake of the kingdom. People made promises on my behalf at my baptism that
I would renounce the evil powers of this world which corrupt
and destroy the creatures of God, and how can I do that if
I keep them always at arm's length, as something other than
myself? How can I recognize the wolves of wrath and darkness
when they're circling if I refuse to admit to nothing more in the

expanse of my own character than a cute and cuddly Shih-Poo? (I could have chosen any dog, and this is the one I went for. You're welcome.)

Cheryl Bridges Johns said, in an interview about her book *The Seven Transforming Gifts of Menopause*:

> I hope that my book will help women develop anger competency and find righteous power in it. Women need permission to be angry, and I'm giving them permission. We need more publications and sermons that help women see anger as the possibility of righteous power.[7]

I share the same hope. I see midlife as a liminal space where God frees us from the things that have bound us for long enough. Menopausal sister in Christ, you will reclaim your courage. You won't be able to prevent yourself from telling all of your own heart. It will burst out of you when you're not expecting it. That boiling maelstrom of rage within you? That restless frustration? That's all the ordinary courage you lost when you were younger, returning in spades, bubbling up and bursting to get out like someone neglected to loosen the cap on a bottle of homebrew. The thing that will save your midlife is finding healthy ways to let the air out gradually, or this is only going to end one way, with an almighty explosion.

An inconvenient truth about the Christian faith (there are so many of them) is that you can't *actually* go around exploding, thrashing about and directing your rage at people, like Darth Vadar indiscriminately waving his light sabre around, chopping people down, left, right and centre, though this is a pleasing image, I will admit. *Apparently*, God frowns upon this type of behaviour, which is another reason for not believing in God, but here we are. We don't get to flail around and cut other people on the broken edges of our anger and pain. I'm sorry to write this because it annoys me more than anyone. That person wanting to roundhouse kick the thrash metal enthusiast on the train? Hello. It's me. I'm also hopping mad that my enemies are loved by God just as much as I am. It's hideous. Foul. But we still have to learn not to pay the anger forward, no matter how hard that might be. Like not disposing of radioactive waste properly, by hanging onto our anger and letting it burst out chaotically, we proliferate the cycle of negativity and keep it going for ever. Give it to God, who knows how to neutralize rage and recycle it into something that can be used safely. This is what we do when the red mist descends.

The image of Jesus cleansing the temple is a helpful reflection for coping with anger. This story appears in all four Gospels and takes place after his triumphant entry into Jerusalem where he has gone to die. He enters the temple with his disciples and is angered that it's being used as a marketplace and for money to be changed, activities that could have taken place outside just as easily. Perhaps Jesus is merely protesting against over-commercialization, a bit like the time my mum lost it in British Home Stores and demanded to speak to the manager because they'd put the Christmas decorations up in October. But his words from Mark 11.17 suggest that his intentions were far broader:

'Is it now written, "My house shall be called a house of prayer for all the nations"? But you have made it a den of robbers.'

'All nations' hints that this is a story about the breadth and inclusive promise of God's love. That God should be for everyone, for all nations (an echo of Isaiah 56.7), and this promise wasn't being fulfilled. The temple was being misused in more ways than one.

The story gets progressively angrier depending on which Gospel writer you read, from the relatively mild Jesus of Luke's Gospel, who efficiently drives out the market sellers and then engages in a spot of teaching, to the Jesus of John's Gospel, who descends with the Die Hard righteous fury of John McClane, armed with a home-made whip. Guess which version I prefer? When I'm so furious that nothing short of actual carnage will satisfy me, this is the Jesus I turn to. One who knows rage and injustice.

I am the temple and I visualize Jesus entering with his corded whip. Lord, I cannot live inside this rage, I tell him. Please take it away. I want to be free of it. Cleanse me as you cleansed the temple. Drive out the robbers and thieves, those things that have stolen my peace and my well-being. Those things that prevent me from doing your will and crowd out everything except this all-encompassing fury, which lays waste all in its path. Cleanse me Lord, like you cleansed the temple. I have nothing to give you right now other than my rage. Take it and make it yours. Rid me of it and let me be free.

Like the two linked stories that we looked at in Chapter 2, the cleansing of the temple forms a sandwich in Mark's Gospel with the one that comes before it, where Jesus curses a fig tree (Mark 11.12–14) because it neglects to provide him with figs. 'May no one ever eat fruit from you again,' he declares, which is a bit unfair on the tree because it wasn't even fig season. Maybe he was just hungry, who knows? It happens to the best of us. We've all been there; you fancy an orange club biscuit but upon reaching into the tin you find that the thieves and robbers (your greedy family) have eaten every last one. You can yell, 'Bring me my corded whip!' while throwing the empty tin across the room, or you can hide a secret stash of orange clubs just for your own personal, future use. Either/or. The third option is to ponder the consequences of Jesus' cleansing of the temple. I want to consider what that means for how we read these passages as one; Jesus curses a tree for not being fruitful and then goes and cusses out the people in the temple, judging them for not using God's house fruitfully. The moral of this story when taken as a whole is that you can't hope to produce good fruit if your temple is a place where nothing grows.

Anger is often a dead-end emotion. We can examine what it's trying to tell us and sometimes the answer might lead to solutions, but due to the hormonal upheaval of menopause, you might feel angry for no good reason at all. What then? Anger isn't always a teacher, sometimes it's just useless fruit, like an apple without seeds, the opposite of the fruit that St Paul promises us the Spirit will cultivate within us (Galatians

5.22–23). That doesn't mean it's worthless, just that without the potential to be productive, it can't sustain us for long. Also, being angry for an extended period of time is a particularly pernicious form of hell. Like sleeping next to a demon or existing at the centre of a tornado. Being incapacitated by impotent rage isn't how we want to spend the second half of our life. That isn't what we're losing our lives to find.

One of the things we might hope to acquire is the fruit of the Spirit that St Paul speaks of to the church in Galatia, but even though midlife is now upon me some aspects of this fruit still continue to elude me – gentleness for one. Common Christian misconceptions of gentleness convince me it must surely be the durian fruit of the Spirit: sickly enough to make me want to vomit. I weary of ideas of gentleness that are used as a stick to beat the non-compliant with; definitions that include being meek, malleable, tame or ineffectual serve no one, particularly middle-aged menopausal women who've had a belly-full of being told to pipe down.

I'm not a gentle person, it's simply not in my DNA or in my nature. I was born flipping things over. I suffer fools unwillingly and I'm often frank to the point of extreme discomfort in a church that prizes politeness over honesty. If gentleness means I must subsume my passion and my fieriness beneath a veneer of mild-mannered politeness, then it's a gift I'd rather not receive. In some translations of Galatians 5, gentleness is rendered as humility, a quality that is a corrective for pride, and speaks of something more than softness or middle-class civility. Humility has an unassuming power that speaks to me of radical gentleness. Not meek, not mild, but quietly, passionately devoted to integrity and decency. To be radically gentle means to tell the truth with courage, consideration, empathy and compassion. That's the kind of gentleness we should hope for, one that refuses to coddle and leaves room for unpalatable truths to be voiced when needed.

Sometimes our anger is both rational and entirely justified. You may know deeper hurts and injuries that can't be easily dealt with, and which may leave you with an intense anger that swamps you and poisons your soul. I'm horribly, intimately acquainted with the typhoon of rage that searing injustice leaves a person with, which is why for me the most repellent sentence in all the Gospels is *pray for your enemies*. This feels impossible when your soul cries out for vengeance. And yet, what is an angry cry for vengeance other than a plea for God to act in its rawest form? *Deal with them God!* Seems to me to be as perfectly valid and sensible a request as me asking my husband to deal with our kids after one of them flushed a Barbie doll down the toilet and another child pooed on it. Clearly, that wasn't a job for me, was it? I no more wanted to deal with that job (pun intended) than I want to address the fury that curdles my guts and freezes my heart. Suddenly, praying for your enemies seems like the only way to move forward.

You've not understood Christ fully until he's dragged you, kicking and screaming blue murder, onto your knees and physically articulated your jaw in prayer like a furious ventriloquist's dummy, and mouthed the words for you to repeat after him. When you've done that, you'll get to your feet afterwards and realize that you can stand a little taller and straighten your shoulders a little bit more, and that the caustic knot in the centre of your gut has unfurled and you will finally be in possession of two great truths: the people who have harmed you are just as human as you are, and you were never meant to carry the weight of that rage all by yourself. You will know as you never did before that God's burden really is light and that the anger was always God's to carry, not yours. Praying for your enemies means to release the poisonous hold they have over you. It means to divorce them, the people, from their awful actions. After you've spent torturous hours on your knees in the company of your enemies in prayer, you can't help but see them as fellow passengers to the grave, as related children of God. And that knowledge will free you, my friend.

Biblical scholar Ellen Davis has written about how when she was a young seminarian she suffered a bitter experience of betrayal by a friend, and so her pastoral theology tutor gave her a list of psalm numbers and advised her to go into the chapel alone and shout them out at the top of her lungs. 'The psalms provided a vent for my anger,'[8] she said, but after repetition they

INVITING ANGER TO PULL UP A PEW

also counselled her to recognize her own fault, specifically the common idolatry that she'd fallen prey to, which Anne Lamott nailed when she said you know you've created God in your own image when he hates the same people you do. (Though, just for the record, God definitely hates Jar Jar Binks because everyone ought to hate that annoying little so and so.)

The psalms recommended by Ellen Davis's tutor were the imprecatory psalms, also known as the cursing psalms. These prayers barely feature in our lectionaries and you won't hear them preached on a Sunday, but they're a necessary resource for our spiritual health and for maintaining the well-being of the church.[9] If you don't have the words to pray for your enemies, praying the angry words of the psalmist is a good place to start:

Pour out your indignation upon them, and let your burning anger overtake them. (Psalm 69.24)

Words that bring our own anger into God's orbit and honestly name what's on our hearts. We wouldn't shy away from bringing to God our sadness, our pain, our worry, or our gratitude, so why not our anger? God can handle it safely even when we cannot.

Angry? Pray.

Frustrated? Pray.

Resentful? Pray.

Choking on blind rage so colossal you could uproot an oak tree? Pray.

I'm reclaiming my anger and I invite you to reclaim yours. It's ours. It's honestly felt and justly earned. When our anger is righteous, it's well meant; it's a natural reaction to unfairness, frustration and resentment, and we won't be deprived of the full force of it. Our God who was moved to fury by injustice tells us that the world is not served by our silence and passivity, by our compliance and our submission. Sometimes, our angry voices are what the world most needs to hear.

Anger stirs, awake once again. The church invites her to have a seat at the table. The church makes room for her, takes her coat, and lets her vent as much as she needs to. And when

Anger has finally run out of steam, when she's had her say and said all that needs to be said, the church looks at her and sees her for what she is and she's given a new name: Peace.

Notes

1 Slee, N., *The Book of Mary* (London: SPCK, 2007). The Kelham Madonna is a sculpture by Alan Coleman, which now resides in Southwell Minster. This line is an extract from Nicola's poem about the sculpture, imagining Mary as completely other and opposite than the compliant, biddable Mary so commonly depicted in literature and other iconography.

2 Bridges John, C., interview by Handley MacMath, T., 'Interview: Cheryl Bridges Johns, Professor of Spiritual Renewal', *Church Times*, 23 October 2020, https://www.churchtimes.co.uk/articles/2020/23-october/features/interviews/interview-cheryl-bridges-johns-professor-of-spiritual-renewal (accessed 26.4.24).

3 Brown, L. Mikel and Gilligan, C., *Meeting at the Crossroads: Women's psychology and girls' development* (Cambridge: Harvard University Press, 1992, p. 75).

4 Rogers, A., 'Voice, Play, and a Practice of Ordinary Courage in Girls' and Women's Lives', *Harvard Educational Review*, 63(3), 1 September 1993.

5 Wesley, J., 'Upon Our Lord's Sermon on the Mount', sermon 22 in *The Works of John Wesley*, Vol. 5 (Grand Rapids: Zondervan, 1958, p. 264), quoted in Low, M., *God, I'm Angry! Anger, Forgiveness, and the Psalms of Vengeance* (Carlisle: Langham Global Library, 2023, p. 17).

6 Luther, M., *What Luther Says: An Anthology*, Vol. 1, compiled by Ewald M. Plass (St Louis: Concordia, 1959, entry nos 28, 29), quoted in Low, *God, I'm Angry!* (p. 17).

7 Bridges John, Interview by Handley MacMath.

8 Davis, E., *Getting Involved with God: Rediscovering the Old Testament* (Lanham: Rowman & Littlefield Publishers, Inc. 2001, p. 24).

9 Davis, *Getting Involved with God* (p. 24).

We lose our way on the fourth day

The things we forget in the fire

We move ever deeper into the wild places, determinedly trudging forward, stopping for short breaks every so often to catch our breath and rest our legs. The road we're travelling on is unfamiliar to all of us and the surroundings are alien even to those who've not been this way before. Emptiness yawns before us, vast and barren, with no landmarks to guide us nor vegetation to break up the monotonous void. Nothing lives here except us women. We roam aimlessly and seemingly without purpose, abandoned like the ninety-nine sheep who remain in the wilderness while the shepherd heads off to look for the one who was lost. We're lost too, and no one seems to care.

We grow hotter as we lumber slowly onwards, not knowing when we'll arrive at our destination or even where it's likely to be. More than one of us starts to fear that the journey will never end. What then? Will we be lost here for ever? This part of the wilderness is a wasteland, where the sun beats relentlessly down causing us to forget everything we ever knew, including ourselves. Thoughts swirl and simmer, and we struggle to make them connect. Meaning flutters on the edges, just out of sight, evading us when we reach for it, like trying to pick fragments of broken shell out of spilled egg white. That's how it is sometimes: every thought is surrounded by sticky, impenetrable gloop and feels impossible to grasp.

We're silent as we walk, needing to concentrate on putting one foot in front of the other. Heat flares within our bodies and radiates outwards, like a pyroclastic flow. If we could glow, we surely would. Sweat pours from our heads and down our necks, gluing our shirts to our backs like a clammy second skin. Our faces blaze like beacons and there's no shade to be found to alleviate the burden of heat, no respite available in this unyielding place. Women fan themselves with their hats, bringing little relief.

'I could have sworn the water-hole was here somewhere,' an elder says, craning her head to see into the distance, where visibility is woeful and wavey with water vapour rising. The air shimmers with heat.

Some of us uncharitably roll our eyes, frustration getting the better of us. One woman suggests we stop for a moment.

'Let's pray,' she says. 'Let's ask God to guide us.'

We drop our bags and sink down onto the dusty ground, where it's slightly cooler though bone hard beneath our bottoms.

'I'll lead us,' the same woman says. And she starts to pray a prayer we've all known since childhood. One that is indelibly etched onto our minds from a thousand repetitions, one that we all know so well we could say it in our sleep.

The woman pauses midway through the prayer, and the silence stretches beyond her merely taking a breath. 'Do you know what? I've forgotten the bloody words,' she says. Our eyes snap open and we all turn to look at her. Hair hangs in wet tendrils about her face, which flames red with the heat and now with embarrassment too. 'Nope. It's gone,' she declares, throwing her arms up in a gesture of frustration and defeat. Someone giggles and then grunts after a quick nudge in the ribs from her neighbour.

'It happens to us all,' an elder says. Heads nod and murmurs of affirmation break the awkwardness. The girl shuffles over to the woman and takes her hand.

'Shall we say the words together?' she asks. 'I remember them.' She settles herself down beside the woman and closes her eyes. Still holding her hand, she starts to pray:

'Give us this day,' she begins, and the woman finds her words again and we all pray along with her.

5

Fever and fog

For my days pass away like smoke,
and my bones burn like a furnace.

Psalm 102.3

Ghandi famously said, 'I like your Christ, I do not like your Christians. Your Christians are so unlike your Christ.' And when I first heard this quote I thought: *I feel that*. I'm as surprised as anyone else that when I became a Christian, I didn't miraculously transform into Christlike perfection, but still. Some of the worst behaviour I've seen from other human beings has been within the confines of the church, and this is why I can't disagree with Ghandi (though while we're all being judgey here, he certainly wasn't perfect either!).

'Why *do* so many Christians suck?' I asked a priest, shortly after I became a Christian myself. He said that the church was like a hospital, and so people who were sick and in need of healing was exactly what I ought to expect to find. Of course, I know now that this priest was riffing off Matthew 9.12, where Jesus says, 'Those who are well have no need of a physician, but those who are sick …' in response to being asked why he chose to hang out with sinners. The priest who shared this insight with me also pointedly said that *some people* were called to be doctors, and this was partly what led me down the path towards ordination. I was far too rubbish at maths at school to ever get the grades needed to be an actual doctor, but I probably would have made a fairly decent nurse. It's in my blood, after all.

'Jayne's started her periods.' It was 1990 and my mother had glibly announced this at the dinner table, just as my dad was reaching for the brown sauce. My older brother feigned deafness. My poor dad, a tattooed, muscly, manly man of few words and a limited understanding of *women's issues*, nevertheless put the sauce down long enough to say: 'Well. That's good then.'

And that was that.

The fact that this wasn't a huge source of embarrassment for me (it might have been for Dad) is something I'm only now, thirty-three years later, coming to fully appreciate. My mum was a gynaecology nurse, a detail that has impacted my life in all sorts of ways, but mostly provides the single greatest explanation for why I am completely comfortable with talking openly about dry vaginas and period clots, to the extent that I forget not everybody was blessed with a mother like mine.

I first learned about menopause when I was a teenager, because if you have your babies in your late twenties, then you'll find yourself facing the thrilling prospect of raising teens at the same time you're facing down perimenopause. My mum was no exception to this generalization. This was in the mid to late 1990s, a time when HRT was demonized and feared as a major cause of breast cancer, a worry that's largely been debunked now. The generation of women who hit perimenopause during this period will have mostly gone the cold turkey, frontier's woman route, enduring with silent stoicism because the option to not do that just wasn't there. Despite this, I envy my mum and her friends their experience, which seemed so much simpler than navigating the barrage of possible symptoms, issues and consequences that we have to grapple with nowadays.

Mum worked on a ward staffed almost entirely by women in their forties, caring for mostly middle-aged or elderly patients. If you were under twenty weeks pregnant and were having bleeding or complications, this is where you went. Ward 12, as the gynae ward was known, was the place to go for all problems involving female biology. Cancers of the womb, cervix, ovaries or vulva. Miscarriages and ectopic pregnancies. Complications due to severe endometriosis. Our haemorrhaging woman from the Gospels would have definitely been brought here if such a place had existed in her time. This tight-knit group of middle-aged nurses, known to one another as the Gynae Girls, worked daily with traumatic events and heart-rending situations, and I find it fascinating that they were all going through menopause at the same time or had already recently been through it.

When Mum talks about her experiences during this time in her life, I get a real sense of deep companionship from her recollections; these women who pressed their fingertips on the damaged cervixes of other women, pulled lost babies from their wombs, smelled the straw-like scent of spilled uterine waters, and were splashed with menstrual blood that flowed without ceasing, couldn't help but be thoroughly cognisant of the messy reality of female biology and how utterly inescapable it is. They were intimately and profoundly connected to women's embodied reality in a unique way, and they formed a sisterhood like no other. And while they probably didn't realize it at the time, they provided a support for one another that most women just don't have access to. Mum told me:

> We were all in the same boat. We had each other's backs and there were no inhibitions. There was an openness and nothing that couldn't be talked about. Hot flushes, weight gain, hairy chins, bad moods, feeling forgetful and foggy. Nothing was taboo.

There's a freedom to this that the church could learn a lot from. No bodily fluid or process was prohibited because it couldn't be. The hospital ward was a place for healing and that could only happen in a spirit of honesty and openness. A house of healing needs to be someplace where we hear the invitation: *show me your wounds and I will help you heal them.* But how can we do this when just mentioning them in passing is a taboo act? If we must sweat and flush with silent shame and pretend it's not happening? I'm not suggesting we ought to free-bleed all over the pews and deliberately make people uncomfortable by shouting out, 'VAGINA!' during the notices, but a little more fluency with openly discussing our own embodiment wouldn't go amiss. More preaching and biblical exploration about how our body stories impact us. More liturgies that honour our physical transitions. More songs and hymns to reference our reality. More openness about our struggles in intercessory prayer. *More* body literacy equals *less* shame.

Certainly, there are parallels between what I've been told by Mum and her friends, and what plenty of Christian women have also shared. Hot flushes represent the biggest bug-bear for lots of menopausal women, making daily life stressful, uncomfortable and anxiety inducing. Priests have told me how unpleasant it is wearing heavy, cumbersome robes which make it impossible to control their temperature; bonus points if the robes are white and you're also struggling with heavy bleeding. Being unable to voice these concerns through a sense of anxiety at how they'll be received can feel very isolating. It can promote a conspiracy of silence that's unhealthy. We bring our whole selves to Jesus to be healed and this includes our hot, sweating, feverish bodies.

Show me your wounds and I will help you heal them.

Let's bring to Jesus that most ubiquitous and archetypical menopause symptom, the hot flush. According to US research, they are defined as an experience of intense warmth, accompanied by sweating, flushing and chills, and can cause a change in heart rate and breathing rate, pressure in the head, and can lead to embarrassment and anxiety. While cross-culturally, midlife women use different language to describe this heat sensation, the fact it's a phenomenon reported across the world in many different societies indicates that hot flushes are a core symptom of menopause.[1]

Across the Atlantic, the hot flush is commonly known as a hot flash, such as that written about by Darcey Steinke in her book *Flash Count Diary*. She writes:

> I flashed while eating a Greek salad at a diner ... I flashed at the Citibank where I got cash and in line at the coffee shop. The worst flash occurred while I was teaching.[2]

In the UK, where flashing means something *very* different, we describe them as flushes because that's exactly what happens: a flush of colour rises from the chest and neck to flame the face, but in truth, this description doesn't really encapsulate the full violence and scope of the sensation that some women report. This is no mere blush, the likes of which I suffered from at school every time the teacher picked on me, a shame made far worse by people pointing and loudly saying, 'You've gone red!' But it does share that common trait of causing the sufferer to feel ashamed. The hot flush announces itself loudly and garishly, screaming: 'This woman is old!' In a culture that mocks and derides ageing, it's a humiliating experience, one best hidden, ignored and not discussed. Hot flushes powerfully announce failing fertility and femininity, unattractiveness and sexlessness. They vividly declare, according to every popular modern metric: this woman is less than. Which is why I often like to imagine Jennifer Lopez having a hot flush and I find that this makes me feel better. Try it for yourself.

In *Flash Count Diary*, Darcey Steinke describes how debilitating and deeply unpleasant she finds them:

> Flames are burning from my inner organs up into my muscles towards the skin. I'd run away but how does one flee one's own body?[3]

This is a sentiment that invokes the words of the psalmist in Psalm 139.7: 'Where can I go from your spirit? Or where can I flee from your presence?' And the comfort to be found in that psalm: 'there your hand shall lead me, and your right hand shall hold me fast' (139.10). The Bible might not refer to hot flushes and menopause specifically, but there is still much wisdom to be found. Scripture is chock-full of references to flames and burning, and not just those that are ostensibly about hell. Being on fire is a spiritual metaphor that we're to understand is a wholly positive one. This is the language of religious fervour and of conversion. Being on fire for God is a sign of spiritual health and renewal.

Ignatian spirituality is replete with this imagery, because reportedly the last words that St Ignatius said to his friend St Francis Xavier as he sent him off to share the gospel were, 'Go set all on fire!' (Said with the confidence of a man who clearly never had to stand naked in front of his open fridge-freezer at 2 a.m., fanning himself with his discarded nightie.)

Researchers into hot flushes think it might not be all bad news. Hot flushes are thought to be caused by decreasing levels of hormones confusing the hypothalamus (the body's control unit for temperature), but recent studies have shown that this struggle to adapt to new conditions might also result in the brain becoming more flexible. Neurological research, using data specifically relating to hot flushes, showed that this flexibility happened each time there was a flush – the brain adjusted.[4] The waves of heat women experience as hot flushes are the brain's attempt to restore equilibrium to changing conditions. It's not just a sign that something's wrong, it's also a sign that something is going right.[5]

Fire burns, kills and destroys, but it also purifies and cleanses, enabling things to start anew. If it's hot enough it can be a refiner's fire, one that burns with enough energy to create something infinitely precious, to purify silver and gold. Burning marks an end but it's also how things get to begin again. My life verse comes from the story of the journey to Emmaus, particularly the line, 'Were not our hearts burning within us while he was talking to us on the road?' (Luke 24.32). It's my life verse (by that, I mean a verse I've chosen through prayer and discernment which speaks to me above all other scripture) because I'm a late convert to the Christian faith and the journey to Emmaus characterizes some of my journey. For me, discovering there was a God began with choosing to step out into the possibility of faith, with curiosity, and was solidified by a dramatic Damascene moment involving a sudden realization of truth. This happened to me one rainy night in the spring of 2012, and afterwards, when I returned home, my husband remarked: 'You look like you've been lit up from the inside out.' Which reminds me not only of what a hot flush looks like to an observer, but also of the Margaret Atwood poem 'Eating Fire', which contains the line, 'to be lit up from within'.[6] I was flushed by the discovery of God.

Since that day, feeling the fire of God burning inside me is something that's comforted me when the world outside has felt cold and dead. If we can just reimagine the burning of menopause as something that is reigniting our call to serve God in new and fresh ways, then we have no need to fear the fire. With every tongue of flame we are being reborn. This might be hard to imagine when you're kicking the sheets off during another sleepless night, but God never promised it would be easy, just that he would be beside us throughout it all, until the end of the age, or at least until air-con is free and mandatory in all households. Breathe on me, breath of God! And make it icy cold please.

There is a story in Matthew's and Luke's Gospels that makes me think of the debilitating nature of hot flushes. It's one of a series of healing stories, where Jesus cures a leper, fixes a paralysed servant, and drives out demons, but this particular story gets lost amid all the razzmatazz of the more miraculous healings. In Matthew 8.14–16 and Luke 4.38–41, there is a short, *blink and you'll miss it* healing involving Peter's mother-in-law (or in Luke's Gospel, the artist formerly known as Simon). This is a woman with an adult child so she's probably middle-aged, and the text tells us that she is lying in bed with a fever. The Greek word that's translated as fever could also mean, *to be on fire*. No other symptoms are given for what ails this woman, other than being hot and sweaty, but what we are told is that Jesus stands close by her, holds her hand, and the fever leaves her and she gets up and serves him.

As a deacon, ordained in God's church to serve, this story of a woman, whose feverish symptoms are rebuked by Jesus and cast off so she can get up and serve God, captures my imagination. The word used in the original Greek text to denote service – *diakonei* – probably wasn't intended to denote diaconal service in an ecclesiastical sense, because it refers to attending to physical needs, but is this in any way a less powerful or valuable way of serving God? The women my mother served with, using their hands to fetch and to carry and ultimately to heal, tell me it's not. The gifts of healing and hospitality are as essential to the kingdom of God as the gifts of preaching and prophesying. It's a story of the equality of Jesus' ministry, giving as it does a glimpse of a fairer social structure, where women were valued members of the team. It's also a situation where someone is laid low with a fiery fever but is touched by Jesus and 'literally rises to the occasion'.[7]

She wakes up and rises to serve Jesus, whereas her son, the rock upon whom Jesus' church will be built, is found sleeping on the job, when Jesus needs him the most (Matthew 26.36–46). One is an example of someone overcoming their physical issues and not letting them get in the way of serving God, while the story that comes later in the garden of Gethsemane is one of giving in, of not being able to stay awake even though Jesus had explicitly said that was what he needed. When Jesus commands us to get up and stay awake, it's not done without good reason.

Of course, serving at midlife would be so much easier if we could only remember what it was that we were supposed to be doing. You know the feeling: you've walked into a room, with purpose and a clear objective, only to come to a standstill, not knowing for the life of you why you're there. Or you're about to lead a service or chair a meeting, and despite the notes you have to hand, you can't remember what it is you're supposed to be saying. Sometimes, you can't recall your own name, let alone anyone else's. Thoughts dance out of reach, requiring massive amounts of concentration to just think clearly and remember simple instructions and details. This is brain fog, a blight of midlife and a commonly noted affliction of menopause, with approximately two-thirds of women reporting difficulties.[8] Another Margaret Atwood poem poignantly describes the increasing frequency of feeling: 'the edges of me dissolve'.[9] It's hard to serve with confidence when sometimes it feels like the you you've known all your life is vanishing daily. That quint-essential question of midlife, 'Who am I now?' is all the harder to answer when your thoughts disperse in the mist and you're denied the clarity of clear thinking.

After a conversation about these menopause woes, my best friend forwarded me an email with a spiritual reflection involving eagles, based on this passage from Isaiah 40.31:

but those who wait for the LORD shall renew their strength; they shall mount up with wings like eagles, they shall run and not be weary, they shall walk and not faint.

The commentary was of unknown provenance, and it talked at length of the moulting process of eagles. Apparently, eagles moult later in life as a result of an accumulation of dirt and oil which over time makes their feathers heavy. Moulting, according to this unknown author, is a way for the eagle to rejuvenate themselves so that they can live a longer life. Just like people, when eagles age they start to wither and lose their former glory; their feathers, beak and talons crack and start to break. To survive, they must shed what is broken and start again. They do this by secluding themselves in a deserted valley, away from potential predators, and then they begin a painful process of plucking out their feathers, breaking off their beaks and talons by smashing them on rocks. Because the process is so gruelling, they're dependent upon their fellow eagles for sustenance while the transformation is taking place, but they emerge afterwards stronger, fitter and sharper than ever.

I so desperately wanted this story to be true. An animal that rejuvenates when it's older! A bird who endures a painful, debilitating transformation but emerges afterwards all the better for it! It was too perfect. Which is why it was, of course, complete and utter bird crap. A cursory fact check confirmed that this was a story that had been doing the rounds via email since the mid-2000s, presumably because it was such a great metaphor for endurance on the Christian journey, but nowhere could I find evidence that eagles deliberately break their talons and beaks in order to regenerate. As with a lot of myths, there are grains of truth to be found. Yes, eagles moult.[10] In fact, they have several moults during their lifetime, and after they've reached sexual maturity, their reproductive systems will shut down during a moult so their energy can go into producing the new feathers. They need this process of renewal to happen so that they can continue to fly; shedding the old to grow anew is essential for their survival.

My favourite way of exploring the Bible is through narrative criticism, a way of studying the text by attending to the stories that are told in order to make meaning of them that can be applied to our lived experiences. The exaggerated nature of this yarn about eagles made me think. So much of popular menopause discourse is full of doom mongering about what women's experiences are likely to be. It's a deficiency. It's a disorder. It's a disease, which unless you medicate yourself to the hilt with hormones you'll never survive. 'No woman can be sure of escaping the horror of this living decay. Every woman faces the threat of extreme suffering and incapacity.'[11] These words from American gynaecologist Robert Wilson, writing in 1966, aren't a million miles away from ones I see every day from current menopause specialists on my social media feeds. They promote a model of menopause that frames it as a hormone deficiency; an accidental quirk of nature that only came about when medical advances lowered mortality, an argument that historian Susan Mattern says should be 'relegated to the garbage heap of scholarship'.[12] The lower mortality rate, which pre-dates twentieth-century advances in medicine, is the result of a hideously low infant mortality rate, which pulls down the average, and not because women didn't live much beyond the age of fifty. Anthropological and historical evidence concludes that women have always had a significant post-reproductive lifespan.[13]

Robert Wilson wrote a book called *Feminine Forever*. He set himself up as a man who was battling a terrible and crippling disease: menopause. This must have been a beguiling argument in the 1960s when the complaints of women were marginalized and unheard. It's a compelling argument still, especially for women who are suffering horribly and who feel like there's nowhere else to turn. Robert Wilson was funded almost entirely by the makers of Premarin and by other hormonal drug manufacturers,[14] but I'm sure this is just a coincidence.

Many women will find help and solidarity from advice they receive online, but many more will feel freaked out by the way the current conversation is going, anxious and fearful about what's in store, nervously examining every ache, pain and gripe against an ever-increasing checklist of potential symptoms. If you think of yourself as defective because you're lacking essential hormones, the future looks bleak: you'll end up a husk of a woman; shrivelled skin, dry hair, atrophied vagina, aching joints, one or two marbles rattling around in your poor menopausal brain. It's something that will undermine you, horribly, to the point that you'll need support from everyone in your life because you won't be able to cope otherwise. Rather than stepping into our power at middle age, with half a lifetime of wisdom and experience under our belts, as men do, current attitudes to menopause encourage a view of midlife women as vulnerable and in need of special support. Menopause is something that will weaken and reduce you, until like the poor beleaguered eagle, you're left bashing your beak against rocks, desperately trying to claw your way to some kind of renewal.

Or not.

What if, like the story of the eagle, the truth of what happens to midlife women is quite different from the stories that have sprung up around it, stories that get passed around and repeated so often they are treated as fact? This is the point where I have to tread very carefully, because I don't want anyone to feel as if their pain or struggles aren't valid. For some people, both will feature as part of their menopause journey. For others, they will barely feature at all, and some lucky souls will sail through the whole thing. But if you expect your experience to be one of smashing your broken pieces against rocks in order to shed your former self, then that's probably what you'll get. I'm not qualified to decide how you manage your menopause, but I do deal in words and I know they have the power to heal or harm. A good Christian ethic of menopause would seek to use language responsibly, with compassion, and would reject pejorative words that cast any woman as deficient or less than her younger sisters.

My lived experience and my faith tell me that women are capable of amazing things and we're stronger than the world tells us we are, and so a model of menopause that labels midlife and older women, however implicitly, as weak and defective is not one I can get on board with. This doesn't mean we must endure suffering without complaint or never ask for help, but it does mean we have agency. Like those *Choose Your Own Adventure* books, we can decide what our narrative will be. Will you choose a story of suffering and weakness, hiding away while you break apart alone, or will you choose to tell a different tale, one of freedom despite adversity? One of surrender and trust? So much is outside our control, but the narrative is still ours to frame how we choose.

I don't know anything about eagles (other than having had a tab open on my laptop for months with the title *Do eagles moult?*) but I have studied the book of Isaiah. This passage about eagles comes from what we think of as the Second Isaiah, an anonymous prophet whose words come to us after the fall of Jerusalem, written to a desperate people in exile in Babylon, where they'd been carted off to as captives. It was written for people surviving in the wilderness of an alien land. People who were lost and had doubts about God's care for them. People who felt far away from all they knew and had started to question whether God was even present at all. Isaiah's message to them in the wilderness, that they will renew their strength and soar like eagles, is one intended to remind them that God still has compassion for them despite their suffering. It's an encouragement to keep going. It's a message of comfort to let them know that throughout it all, God will see them home safely. It's a promise of restoration.

Menopause may well hold us captive but God wants to set us free. The image of the eagle, who sheds its older self so that it can still have the ability to fly, is one of strength through adversity, persistence through pain, steadfastness through suffering, courage through conviction. It's a symbol of independence and freedom, given by God, who wants us to run and not be weary, walk and not be faint. God, who gives us our wings so that we might soar.

She got up and she served.

With her strength renewed by Jesus, healed, even if momentarily from the fever that threatened to incapacitate her, she got up and she served. She didn't give up. She acknowledged her worth in the eyes of Jesus, her value to his ministry, the contribution that she alone made to serving him, and she got up. Jesus stood close to her, and he took her hand. Maybe he used the same words that he'd later use to raise the girl from the dead. 'Woman, I say to you, arise!' Whatever he said, it worked, because Jesus rebukes our despair. Our pain. Our discomfort. He rebukes it and commands it to leave.

Women, we are not defective. The only thing we need be deficient in are the expectations of a youth-obsessed culture that says we have no worth. We know we are exactly as God made us to be. Let's *get the hell up* and stand tall. Staying down is not an option. We've been kept down long enough. By sexist and ageist attitudes that have defined us as less than. By ourselves, gripped as we so often are by imposter syndrome, or paralysed by politeness that keeps our lips sealed shut lest we offend, or keeps us in a narrow lane, unheard and unseen. If we just carry on as we've always done, then I wonder what we're even waking for. This is our heritage as women of God. A diaconate of all believers. We were made to serve God and to serve each other.

Wipe the sleep from your eyes. Jesus has work for you to do. Let's get up and serve him, and upon the wings of eagles we will fly. Jesus is standing close by and he holds our hands.

Notes

1 Mattern, S., *The Slow Moon Climbs: The Science, History and Meaning of Menopause* (Princeton: Princeton University Press, 2019).

2 Steinke, D., *Flash Count Diary: A New Story about the Menopause* (Edinburgh: Canongate Books, 2019, p. 20).

3 Steinke, *Flash Count Diary* (p. 4).

4 Steinke, *Flash Count Diary* (p. 20).

5 Steinke, *Flash Count Diary* (p. 19).

6 Atwood, M., *Eating Fire: Selected Poetry 1965–1995* (London: Virago, 1998, p. 181).

7 Levine, A.-J., in Newsom, C. A. and Ringe, S. H. (eds), *The Women's Bible Commentary* (London: SPCK: 1992, p. 256).

8 Gunter, J., *The Menopause Manifesto: Own Your Health with Facts and Feminism* (London: Piatkus, 2021).

9 Atwood, from the poem 'More and More', *Eating Fire* (p. 49).

10 This was from an article I read about bald eagles, https://hayfarmguy.com/do-eagles-molt (accessed 1.7.24). I didn't pursue finding out about golden eagles, which are indigenous to Iraq, the modern geographical context for the Babylon of the second book of Isaiah, as this was taking me way off-piste! If anyone wants to look into the moulting habits of golden eagles, please do knock yourselves out.

11 Wilson, R., *Feminine Forever* (New York: W. H. Allen, 1966).

12 Mattern, *The Slow Moon Climbs* (p. 19).
13 Mattern, *The Slow Moon Climbs* (p. 27).
14 Mattern, *The Slow Moon Climbs*.

We find flowers in the wilderness on the fifth day

And he called the dry land good

Last night we made camp at the summit of a cliff, so we could enjoy the view of the sun coming up in the morning from on high. We endured a difficult, slow climb to get to the top, but the end result was more than worth the hard work to get us here. The Elders promised us this would be the case and we're so glad we listened. We've learned to follow their lead as they show us places they remember, familiar landmarks and treasured views. We're grateful for their wisdom.

'It will be a tiring journey, hot and uncomfortable, but you'll be so pleased you made the effort,' they said. They were right. Exhausted after the climb, we didn't linger long at the campfire, and instead made for our beds early, so we could wake when it was still dark. Huddled together in our blankets, we sat on the edge of the cliff in a row and watched the sun rise over the mountains and up into the clouds, which were soon burned off and dispatched by the encroaching orange light, which spread gradually over the landscape like the questing fingertips of God.

Today, the dome of the sky stretches above us, an unfathomable embrace of endless blue. Creatures of the firmament swoop and glide, showing us what it looks like when you give in to the possibility of freedom. Our small camp hums gently with the sounds of early morning activity. The hiss and crackle of the fire. The metallic rattle of the pans and enamel cookware. The buzz of zippers as tent flaps open and close. The gentle chatter of greetings and grumbles. Some mornings we have begun our day by searching through the foliage for wild chamomile or mint to brew tea, but here on this isolated clifftop nothing appears to grow. The ground below our feet is scorched by the sun; parched and dry, a carpet of cracked brown dust, scattered with rocks, with no greenery to relieve its barren monotony.

There will be no fresh tea this morning. No apples to have with our oats. There are no trees or bushes where we can pick berries. No wild sustenance to be found here. Here, nothing grows. Here, all is dead. The ground, which may have been fertile once, now looks all but spent. The good vibes we enjoyed as we watched the beauty of the sun rise slowly start to fade and a mild depression settles over us like a grey blanket. Our invigoration dwindles with the dawn. How can anything good and vital come from a place where nothing appears to grow?

'Over here!' a high-pitched voice cries. 'Come and see what I've found!'

The girl calls us from the far side of the cliff, where she's wandered off to on her own. Amid the busyness of the morning, she's been left unsupervised and has drifted too close to the edge.

'Come away from there!' someone yells. The girl lies on her belly, her face pressed close to the ground and with her arms dangling over the rocky edge, and she doesn't appear to hear us calling her. She raises her head and excitedly call us again. 'Look!' she cries. We unwillingly go over to see.

'She probably wants to show us another weird-shaped rock,' one woman grumpily mumbles.

'Look!' the girl repeats, her small round face shining with excitement. She sits back on her haunches and points to the edge in front of her. Cautiously, we peer over. There, sprouting determinedly from a parched crevice, above a dizzying drop, high up off the ground, is a single flower. It has delicate yellow petals but a sturdy green stem, and it springs stubbornly up from a place where nothing else grows, where nothing *ought to grow*, and yet somehow it blooms. Against all expectations, it flourishes amid a wilderness where nothing seems to grow and still it puts forth beauty into the world.

'See?' the girl says proudly, her little face shining with pleasure. 'Just because things seem desolate, hope grows. You just have to look closely for it.'

6

Lifting the tent flaps
for the *over forties*

Sarah laughed to herself, saying,
'After I have been completely dried out,
will there yet be for me wetness?'[1]

My friend is training to be a vicar in the Church of England and she recalls being told by a senior male colleague at a training day that women are 'in their prime' when they are in their late thirties. This meant that my friend, who is intelligent, hard-working, wise and kind, and, like the majority of women in churches, over the age of forty, would be well past this sell-by-date by the time she was ordained and running her own church. That this was said at all raises a few issues, but that it was said by a man who himself was in his fifties is staggering. First, it was delivered with the confidence of it being axiomatic. In other words, he expected the listeners, a mixed cohort of trainee ministers, to agree with him. Second, and perhaps more alarmingly, it hints at what the attitude is from some men in the church; if this is what is said publicly, imagine what's being said privately amid like-minded friends. Lastly, writing this has reminded me that I need to pray for God to smite this man, forthwith.

This little anecdote is no surprise to midlife women, who, as soon as we hit forty, start to feel the contempt that the world has for us, a casual disdain that creeps over into attitudes within the church. This might come as a disappointing surprise to younger women, who already experience misogyny and sexism, to hear that these don't disappear when you get older. You're not instantly regarded as a respected elder of the faith, with wisdom to impart and experiences to share. No, ageism gets added to the mix as well, because when you reach your forties, you become classified as *not young* any more, which usually just means that in ways you can't quite put your finger on, your value has diminished.

The church is obsessed with courting and sustaining the attention of youth, because the young are seen as the only viable way for the church to grow and achieve new life, so you'll barely even register as being significant to the statistics if you're over forty. I've lost count of the number of times someone in the church has referred to the *over forties* with a snidey pejorative edge added to it, a tone that immediately makes me reimagine myself as being as torpid and decrepit as Charlie Bucket's grandmas. A bit mouldy and irrelevant. Nothing useful to contribute. Faintly embarrassing. Taking up space in the middle of everything with my giant iron bedstead. The disconnect is confusing. Inside, I'm still young and vital, a main character who is integral to the storyline, but some sections of the church make me feel as if I ought to be taking to my room and donning a frilly mop cap like Mrs Bennet, screaming shrilly about my nerves, while everyone downstairs rolls their eyes and argues about who has to bring me my tea.

To add credence to the disparaging stereotype, whenever a famous *over forties* woman appears in public not resembling a toothless, sexless old hag, the astonishment that abounds is very telling: 'She's fifty!' The tabloids and social media exclaim in shock, as if she's performed a miraculous trick: *'And she has all her own teeth and isn't even using a hearing trumpet, it's amazing!'* We marvel at how the celebrities with their glamorous, top-end lifestyles all seem to coincidently also be genetically advantaged when it comes to ageing, which is why when I'm giving myself my morning pep talk in the mirror, I always make sure to say: 'Remember: you're not fat and old, Jayne. You're just skint.'

The more I read about how midlife famous women are treated by the press and by the ad hoc reckons of people on social media, the more I'm glad I don't share their supposed good fortune. Take supermodel Kate Moss for example, a woman who has made her living from her beautiful face and body, and who has recently turned fifty:

> When Kate Moss wakes up on Tuesday 16 January, she will open her eyes to the first day of her sixth decade. As most women will attest, turning fifty is a significant milestone that can be somewhat daunting. But while many women in the public eye insist that reaching midlife and menopause is to be celebrated, it is unlikely that Kate will see it this way.[2]

If you didn't read this in the style of David Attenborough describing the final moments of the last rhino in Africa, then please do so now. Portentous and doom-laden words for a woman who is – *checks notes* – becoming one day older. To amuse myself, I googled 'Daniel Craig at fifty' just to see if the same pessimistic nonsense had been written about him. In news that will surprise no one, I discovered a plethora of articles with titles such as 'How Daniel Craig became the fittest 50 year old on the planet',[3] plus plenty of pictures of him in his pants. (I took one for the team on this, because I don't want to be responsible for causing other sisters to stumble. Trust me, I'm a deacon.) There were no hit pieces lamenting him reaching this crumbling milestone, nor any articles pondering how it might be affecting his emotional well-being. Which isn't to say that men aren't adversely affected by the ageing process, just that the world is less affected by it than it is by the ageing of women, which seems to gross people out.

Back to Kate Moss, because wait: there's more!

> It cannot be easy for Kate. Midlife is often particularly poignant for women with daughters as they are forced to watch them blossom while their own bloom fades.[4]

We're to understand that, like Snow White's wicked stepmother, midlifers resent the beauty of young women because it reminds us of our own decay. And while this might be true if you've bought into the lie that your only value and worth is to be found in staying young, it's mostly a nasty trope that serves no other purpose than to divide women and set us up in opposition with one another. Older women have a wealth of experience and wisdom to impart and can be a huge source of pastoral support for younger women, and I'm suspicious of a culture that seems determined to drive a wedge between us.

If given the chance, midlife women can share what we've learned from half a life in the trenches. We might build strong, unbreakable bonds that help develop resilience in the young, breathe new life into the old, and give us all the communal courage to resist and reject sexism whenever it threatens to harm women and girls. But if no one wants to listen to us because we're assumed to be embittered old harpies, then nobody benefits. Midlife women also need the support of their elders, particularly while trying to navigate bodily processes long shrouded in mystery, such as menopause. This is especially important for women who lack family support. Approaching the menopause without a mother, for example, can feel like traversing Scafell Pike without a map. The unique inter-generational social composition of the church should have an invaluable role to play in nurturing strong relationships, but not if we just reiterate age-old cultural biases.

The idea of having a prime is one thing we can bin off, for starters. According to dictionary.com, *past one's prime* means to be 'beyond the peak of one's powers', and reading this made me send up another prayer to ask God to hurry along with that smiting I requested. How dare anyone suggest that a woman is beyond the peak of her powers if she's over forty? If this is our peak then the human race is doomed, starting with the church, which is run by and populated with women who are not only past this summit, but all the way down the other side of it.

This is another reason why the church needs to reject popular notions of menopause which encourage the idea it's a life stage that fundamentally damages and weakens women. If we want to push back against sexist stereotypes of women being past the peak of our powers after forty, then conversations about menopause as a deficiency, or worse, a disease, however well intended, are ultimately unhelpful. I can't be the only woman in her forties who's been made to feel panicky by the current messaging and online advice that's available, the vast online checklists of symptoms being a major source of anxiety.

For example, the symptoms on a popular online *Menopause Symptom Checklist* include the following: feeling tense or nervous, difficulty sleeping, joint and muscle pain, having trouble concentrating, memory problems, feeling tired or lacking in energy, irritability and headaches, among others. I've also seen checklists of symptoms that include everything from a flaky scalp to a dry mouth to restless legs to indigestion, constipation, the runs, watery eyes, dry eyes and Blue Puffin Disorder (OK, that last one might not be true). I'm obviously not a doctor (and if I were one, I'd be a menopause specialist, because that appears to be a hugely popular and lucrative business to be in right now), but just a quick glance at this one checklist alone tells me that these symptoms might have another, far more obvious cause and it's one that afflicts both men and women: it's called getting older. In fact, my husband scored highly enough on this checklist to make me worry that he might be perimenopausal, and that was even with him firmly rejecting vaginal dryness and hot flushes.

I'm not suggesting these symptoms can't be a sign of perimenopause, and nor do I want to diminish anyone's suffering, but since menopause occurs at a time when we will probably also be experiencing the signs of ageing, it's really important that women don't falsely attribute every pain and symptom to declining hormones.[5] It's not clear-cut at which point individual women enter the perimenopause phase, since tests that determine hormone levels aren't a reliable indicator. This is why we fall back on checklists to flag possible symptoms, which can be enormously helpful, except that women who already believe their symptoms are caused by perimenopause are more likely to report them as such.[6]

I'm of the opinion that if you think like a hammer, then everything will look like a nail, or in other words, if the current menopause conversation has you on high alert that this might be a factor, then every twinge, sign and change starts to be attributable to it. And before you stop reading and throw this book across the room in disgust (that'll be that rage we've discussed) let me repeat – emphatically – my wholehearted conviction that whatever you think you need to do to feel better, you must crack on and do it. I've met enough women who believe that hormone therapy has alleviated their symptoms and made life that little bit more bearable, to make me think that hormone therapy is definitely worth pursuing for some people. I want to insist though that we reject every hint that women are in any way labelled deficient without the same levels of hormones we had when we were younger. I simply don't believe that this is true.

If you've imbibed current menopause folklore, which decrees that you're lacking and afflicted by a debilitating disease, then how does this combat ageing in an ageist society? Regarding menopausal women as defective compared to younger women does a disservice to us all. It demonizes ageing and makes it something to be feared, which in turn further erodes the bonds between generations which are crucial for our sense of belonging. It robs older women of their inherent value as elders and sacred bearers of God's image. Most of all, it dishonours God who surely knew what he was about when creating us and didn't expect us to be thrown on the scrapheap at age fifty.

The veneration of health and youth as virtues is a pervasive idolatry of our culture, and one that the church must strenuously reject. As well as being ageist it's also hugely ableist. This shouldn't need pointing out, but health (a nebulous concept anyway) is not a metric of our worth. Our inherent value as children of God does not come from how healthy and young we are. Specifically, when we're speaking of bodies that go through menopause – a process that by design brings about infertility – we need to assert in the strongest possible terms that human value does not come from our ability to reproduce. Young people who suffer with infertility, both male and female, particularly need to hear the church speak this truth, because the harm that's caused by assigning special virtue to parenthood is an upsetting reality that marginalizes those without children. The lionization of motherhood as the summit of all female ambition also creates a wound that can get reopened during menopause for women who wanted to have children but were never able to. Menopause is a definitive ending that can be starkly painful in its finality.

Infertility is something that the biblical record contains numerous examples of, but I'm most interested in the stories of those women who were also post-menopausal, such as Sarah, the wife of Abraham, and Elizabeth, the mother of John the Baptist. The patriarchal society they lived in, one that relied on male descendants to carry legacies forward and to replenish and bolster family units in brutally hard times, had one main use for women and that was the birthing of children. If they didn't fulfil this role then lifelong blame and shame was theirs. And yet, scripture tells us that God didn't see these women as defective or past their prime, but as a means by which God's purposes would be fulfilled. The fact that these women are post-menopausal tells us that God views older women as worthy of being repositories of new life. Rather than being off-stage and not part of the action, we're shown that older women have an integral part to play in the drama of God.

Let's focus on the story of Sarah, from the book of Genesis. She's described as 'advanced in age' (Genesis 18.11), but this doesn't neatly map onto modern standards of ageing, and the record of her life comes from a disparate range of sources, so it's doubtful it reflects an accurate chronological narrative.[7] Plus, her story comes to us from a time that lacked the subtlety of transitional delineations, such as the absence of a teenage phase between child and adulthood and no recognizable concept of midlife either. The main distinction that exists is between fertile and no longer fertile, the difference between menarche and menopause. For this reason, I see Sarah as being a good archetype for midlife women since she's clearly regarded as not being reproductively useful but is still active and functioning as the female head of the household, wielding relatively high status in her community as the wife of a wealthy man.

Sarah (or Sarai, as she's known when we first encounter her) is the childless wife of Abraham (Abram) and Hagar is her Egyptian maid servant whom she presses into service as a surrogate so her husband can have an heir. It's a story about social rivalry, showing us what happens when a more powerful woman abuses a lower-status woman in her care. It details the mess that ensues when patriarchy warps the bonds between women. Womanist theologians also see the story of Hagar and Sarah as being emblematic of how racial inequality can divide us, such as Renita Weems, who writes:

> Injustice in our land relies upon perpetual alienation of women from one another and upon relentless hostility among women.[8]

I see this story also as one involving a generational conflict, a tale of the gulf between young and old. The text tells us that Sarah is post-menopausal: 'it had ceased to be with Sarah after the manner of women' (Genesis 18.11), whereas Hagar is presumed to be fertile and so therefore is still young. The perception of Hagar's body is one that is vital and productive, while Sarah's is purposeless and barren. No wonder she feels desperate enough to take matters into her own hands.

Sarah's reaction, while being a product of her time, tells us so much of how we too can feel despair at how the world treats bodies that it deems to serve no productive purpose or which it doesn't understand: disabled bodies, queer bodies, fat bodies, damaged bodies. Maybe your own experience intersects with some of these things and the world sees only your broken body and not you at all, and you worry that menopause will diminish your value further. Sarah's world saw only her barren body and this was an inescapable reality for a woman of her time.

Her encounter with God is one of my favourite passages in all of scripture because while she's a relatively passive participant in the action, she does something that isn't recorded often in the Bible: she laughs. In Genesis 18, Abraham is visited by three mysterious guests, a meeting apparently with the divine.

It's such an evocative piece of scripture; I imagine Sarah standing at the entrance to the tent with Abraham, watching the three figures approach through a haze, silhouetted against the descending sun, the image blurry with heat rising from the ground. I feel her anxiety in the frenetic activity of having to cook and prepare a meal for these unexpected but honoured guests. I smell the roasted meat and the baking bread. I feel Sarah, hot and sweaty inside the tent, straining her ears to hear the extraordinary conversation taking place outside the canvas. She, a post-menopausal woman, will bear a son. She, whose womb has not cramped in years, will carry a child. She, who has completely dried out, will once again have wetness.[9] Her response is to laugh. No wonder!

The NRSV translation of Sarah's response is, 'After I have grown old, and my husband is old, shall I still have pleasure?' (Genesis 18.12), a passage that Jewish biblical scholar Nahum Sarna renders as 'abundant moisture' instead of pleasure, which, as Wilda Gaffney points out, is a really bold acknow-ledgement of the sexual desire of women.[10] This is a topic that you'll rarely find talked about openly, but it's hugely pertinent to a discussion about menopause, because vaginal dryness is one of the symptoms that women are known to suffer from, starting at midlife and beyond, and is a source of silent shame. As many as 15% of women report symptoms, which rises to 80% when women are post-menopausal and elderly.[11] The changes women describe can cause real distress; this isn't just a case of not wanting to have sex any more. A lack of oestrogen, decreasing collagen and a gradual reduction in blood flow, over time cause shrinkage of the vaginal tissues and a decrease in lubrication, which can lead to pain and discomfort.[12]

We can assume that at her advanced age, Sarah has experi-enced all these things, but I still find it fascinating that her response isn't to say, 'How will I conceive a child?' or 'How will I carry a child?' No, her chief concern is closer to the bones of the matter; she wonders how it will be possible for her body to experience desire again. It's beyond the scope of my research to ponder how Abraham, who is older than Sarah, might still be able to get it on despite his great age, because after all, as Dr Jen Gunter says, 'it's a penis, not a magic wand',[13] but I digress. Sarah laughs and God responds: 'Is anything too wonderful for the LORD?'

Sarah's story has long been read as a message of optimism for the childless; an encouragement that God eventually answers prayers if we wait long enough. But when read through the lens of menopause, we see different things. It's an encouragement not to give up hope, even when the world sees us as defunct and redundant as a boarded-up high street, God sees us as repositories of new life. Sarah isn't an icon of motherhood, she's a symbol that the only pathway to new life is through trusting in God. She's a witness to the truth that what the world sees as dried up and barren, God sees as a place of fresh possibility. Just like the creation story in the first chapter of Genesis, *God called the dry land good*. It was a place where things would still grow. I read Sarah as a story of rebellious hope in response to ageing.

The potential for pleasure in our lives shouldn't be contingent on whether or not we are fertile. Tying fertility to womanhood as a marker of value and esteem hurts young women particularly, but it does no favours at all to midlife women either, whose loss of perceived value is a direct effect of their loss of fertility. God wants to tell us that older women can be the repositories for new life, because they have the potential to rewild and regrow new possibilities. Menopausal bodies are a place of rebirth.

The point of the story isn't to reassure women that we'll still be getting jiggy with it after midlife, because sex doesn't have to be a big deal for everyone, and not all women have a partner or want one. That said, it might help some of us to know that research has shown that women who believe that sexual enjoyment will decrease with menopause and ageing are twice as likely to experience a decrease in desire than women who don't share that belief.[14] *Will I still have pleasure* is a really valuable, hope-laden question to ask, and if there's one thing we need as midlife women in a climate where ageing is thought to be damaging even to super-beautiful sirens like Kate Moss, then we need to retain our sense of hope. Frame of mind during menopause counts for a lot and, as Sarah demonstrates, we need to keep laughing. It might just be the thing that saves us.

I'm looking forward to living a life that's unencumbered by a twenty-eight-day cycle and the hormonal upheaval that's tied to it. I'm determined that my midlife will be spontaneous and fun. I will dare to still feel defiantly good about myself even if I have to convince the world that sweaty red faces and chin hair are the sexiest thing since Ursula Andress walked out of the sea in *Dr No*. (Or I'll start a fundraiser for laser removal, whichever comes first.)

I invite every midlife woman reading this to join me in being stubbornly joyful. We will care less what people think of us and we will pursue our own desires and preferences in a way we've never felt brave enough to claim when we were younger. We will use our wisdom to make wise and firm choices, without the dithering and people pleasing that marked our younger years. We will build stronger relationships with other women who have travelled this road with us and who know each marker along the way. We will not remain hidden, overhearing God from behind the tent flaps, because even if the world thinks we need to stay hidden under the canvas we will bring the things that matter to us into the light, including our whole selves. God has a message that's just for us. The promise of new growth in a place that appears lifeless. Of a wellspring bubbling up in ground that the world thinks of as dry and barren. A thirst that will be quenched. Good soil that will seed a new creation.

I know why Sarah laughed. I know how it sounded. It was one of those honking laughs that's ignited by disbelief. A spontaneous guffaw. A sarcastic sound that is actually an affront to real laughter. It's the kind of laugh I imagine I'd have given if I'd heard that guy tell me I'm past my prime. The way you laugh when you've heard something preposterous. Eventually, Sarah gives birth to real laughter.[15] To new life. 'God has brought laughter for me,' she says, 'everyone who hears will laugh with me' (Genesis 21.6).

If nothing is too wonderful for the Lord, then let's pray that midlife will be a time for us to claim our God-given potential to create and seed new life and that we live it, with real laughter. The kind that makes you wonder if Tena Lady might be a feature of your life after all. The kind of laughter that makes you bend over and hold onto your sides. The kind of laughter that only comes from a woman who knows her own worth, who knows her rightful place in the world, and who knows the love of a God who laughs along with her.

Notes

1 Genesis 18.12, as translated by Wilda Gaffney in *Womanist Midrash: A Reintroduction to the Women of the Torah and the Throne* (Louisville: Westminster John Knox Press, 2017, p. 36).

2 Hicks, P., 'Kate Moss at Fifty: Why she is finding ageing harder than her own Mossy Posse', https://www.independent.co.uk/life-style/kate-moss-50-mossy-posse-primrose-hill-midlife-b2476887.html (accessed 26.4.24).

3 Thorp, C., 'How Daniel Craig Became the Fittest 50-Year-Old on the Planet', *Men's Journal*, 20 April 2020, https://www.mensjournal.com/health-fitness/how-daniel-craig-became-the-fittest-50-year-old-on-the-planet (accessed 26.4.24).

4 Hicks, 'Kate Moss at Fifty'.

5 Gunter, J., *The Menopause Manifesto: Own Your Health with Facts and Feminism* (London: Piatkus, 2021).

6 Mattern, S., *The Slow Moon Climbs: The Science, History and Meaning of Menopause* (Princeton: Princeton University Press, 2019).

7 Gaffney, *Womanist Midrash*.

8 Weems, R. J., *Just a Sister Away: Understanding the Timeless Connection Between Women of Today and Women in the Bible* (New York: Hatchette, 2007, e-book, Loc 350).

9 Gaffney, *Womanist Midrash* (p. 36).

10 Sarna, N., in Gaffney, *Womanist Midrash*.

11 Gunter, *The Menopause Manifesto*.

12 Gunter, *The Menopause Manifesto*.

13 Gunter, *The Menopause Manifesto* (p. 164).

14 Gunter, *The Menopause Manifesto* (p. 196).

15 The son whom Sarah bears is called Isaac, which means *one who laughs*.

We grieve on the eve of the last day

A new name I give you

It's our last night together and we feel strangely sad and uneasy. Unspoken grief gnaws at us like hunger pains. The evening has the peculiarly charged feel of Holy Saturday, combining the sorrow of being forced to confront the things we're leaving behind with the tentative expectation of something significant coming with the dawn. There's no way around it: Before resurrection comes death. This is what transition feels like. This is the story of our faith.

We sit once again around the campfire, shawls and blankets around our shoulders and covering our laps, fingers curled round mugs of hot chocolate and steaming tea. We who are on the threshold of midlife have choices to make. This life change will come whether we want it to or not, and it's up to us to decide whether we will meet it as a gift or as a trial. Maybe it's both. Tonight, we will honour this liminal moment with prayer and liturgy, giving thanks and praise for all that has been and all that will be. We are privileged to be here and that is a gift all by itself.

In front of us sits a collection of objects that we've gathered on our journey through the wilderness, and the meanings are personal to each one of us, symbolizing what our menopause and our midlife means to us. The feather, providing the mechanism for flight and freedom, but to some of us it's also emblematic of the empty nest that so often characterizes this phase of life. It's also a symbol of the eagle, of strength and renewal. We each have a smooth and perfectly shaped pebble; a rock to symbolize our foundations in God, and our own steadfastness and fortitude to have made it this far. The rock shows we are hardy and that we know how to endure. Some of us have contributed a poppy seed head, the remains of the flower that once bloomed, but still plump and rounded with the pregnant possibility of new life. It speaks of potential. It symbolizes the rewilding of our middle years. Finally, a flask of crisp, pure water signifies the wellspring from which we drink deep. This is our offertory.

As some traditions do at the sacrament of confirmation or when being received into holy orders, we are invited to choose a new name to claim for our own at this next life stage.

I choose Sophia. She who stands at the crossroads and speaks unpalatable truths. She who personifies God's wisdom and creative power. Other women choose Elizabeth, or Sarah, or Naomi, or Mary. Some women choose Anna because she stayed until the job was done. She remained faithful in the temple until she could show the world who Jesus was. This is the hope for many of us. That we remain despite it all.

Each of us writes our new name on our pebbles and we place them amid the kindling of the fire we light. Into the fire we place other objects that represent what we are leaving behind. Mistletoe for fertility. Daisies for youth. Hyssop to symbolize that like the plants we burn in the fire, we too are being purified.

As the curls of smoke rise up into the air, one woman starts to sob. 'I don't want this,' she cries. 'I want to still be young. All I can think of is the time I've lost. The things I've never seen. The things that will never happen now.' This last is said on a broken sob, and she presses her hand to her belly, her eyes squeezed shut with pain. We rush to comfort her, falling over one another as we shuffle closer to hug her or place a caring hand on her shaking shoulders. She weeps without restraint and we cry with her without words because this is a tender ache that nothing spoken can relieve the pain of. We sit together, our silent weeping the only sound.

'I'm sorry,' the woman sniffs, wiping her eyes with the heels of her hands. 'I didn't mean to upset everyone, it's just that I feel so sad, even after all these years.'

A pair of bony arms encircles her neck, and a small face burrows into her chest. 'I know,' the girl whispers. 'I'm here.'

7

Making sense of the middle

'We walked where there was no path.'[1]

It ended and started with water and blood gushing forth. Water, the liquid of life, mingled with blood, fluid of death. It started while he was still nailed to the cross. His mother Mary witnessed the soldier piercing his side with a spear, one more act of desecration on the flesh that she had loved so well. She felt the pain of it in her soul, just like she'd been promised long ago. What of the other promises that had been made? The bringing of light. The reigning for ever. The kingdom with no end. Oh, how different the favour of the Lord looks when standing in the shadow cast by the cross! There is no hint of resurrection here in this place where 'meaning is dead. Hope is dead. Love is dead.'[2] In the wake of death we must contend with the pain that remains. While the water and blood gush forth.

Holy Saturday is the name the church gives to the day between Good Friday and Easter Sunday, the day between Christ's death and his resurrection, and it's a time to grapple with what it's like to live a life after death when you don't know that resurrection is coming. It's sacred ground from which to observe what was, what is, and what will be. It provides a brutal backdrop to a central, everlasting truth: we cannot go back. What is dead stays dead.

It's possible to see menopause as a kind of resurrection, a process of awakening that involves death followed by new life. The death of youth and fertility, and the rebirth that comes after, where women enter a new reality and a new way of being. But even if we eventually rise with the dawn to a new life, even if we choose to see our menopausal bodies as our resurrected selves, what was lost stays lost. The death of our younger selves is for ever. Placing these experiences within the setting of Holy Saturday challenges us to sit with the pain of death while we decide what to do with what endures.

Resurrection, as it's often referenced in Christian iconography and tradition, is a triumphalist event. 'Up from the grave he rose again!' Stuart Townend sings *In Christ Alone*,[3] conjuring up an image of Christ leaping from the tomb and pumping his fist in the air and maybe even doing a few sparring air punches, like Rocky after he's run up the steps in front of the Philadelphia Museum of Art. But Christ's reappearance amid the dirt and dead things in the garden, an incongruity that made him unrecognizable to even a close friend, hints that the true nature of his resurrection was far more understated. Think mournful kazoo toot, rather than a trumpet blast. This is as it should be, because we don't get to joyfully proclaim that Christ is risen without first paying our respects to the inconvenient, yawning emptiness of the day that comes before. Bearing witness to Holy Saturday is part of our task as Christian disciples. This is how we tell the truth about the faith that we proclaim; that there is no joy without sorrow. No light without dark. No pleasure without pain. We pay attention to the middle places, where dappled light mingles with shadow.

Midlife is the waypoint in the journey of being where we confront those things that have gone. Old grievances. Past traumas. Ghosts from long ago which come back to haunt us. New pains that revive ancient hurts. Our present situation can't help but remind us of our own mortality, because midlife is the brow of a hill where we can see how far we've climbed but now we also have a view of the valley below which marks where the journey ends. We can't help but confront that slowly, *slowly*, we are dying. We always were, of course, but midlife opens up a new way of truly knowing. It's no surprise that this realization can bring about despair and exacerbate existing tensions and strains.

There's an increased risk of depression during the menopause transition, possibly caused by the hormonal maelstrom that occurs, because oestrogen provides a boost for serotonin, its decline messes with the management of mood and memory.[4] However, this isn't the only factor at play. Women who enter the menopause early, before the age of forty-five, are thought to be at increased risk and have higher rates of depression. Other risk factors include a history of traumatic events (particularly in childhood), lack of sleep, inadequate support, and other social causes such as stress or poverty.[5] Interestingly, women who have a negative attitude towards ageing and menopause are at greater risk also, which is inconvenient because it's hard to have a positive attitude when everywhere you look is age-based negativity! Changing the cultural mindset around ageing and menopause would probably have encouraging health benefits, as well as being the right thing to do because Midlife and Older Women are Bloody Amazing and Should be Celebrated (which was, by the way, the working title of this book).

Depression is a veil that prevents us from seeing that resurrection might be possible, a Holy Saturday without an end. Resurrection in this context is messy. It doesn't look victorious. It's characterized by sadness and clawing desperation, because it's been wrenched from a place where beginning again was thought to be impossible. That's the kind of new life we're talking of when we envision it after a stint in the wilderness dogged by depression. If the experience also includes living with trauma then it will always bear the scars of what came before; it will always be marked by the remains of death. Those of us who are forced to abide in Holy Saturday, and who have plundered the depths of its abyss, truly know the wasteland chasm between cross and resurrection. Living with trauma is like carrying a cross that you can't put down. The event that caused the trauma may have ended but you're still marked by it, like splinters festering under the skin.

I've often felt that church liturgy struggles to fully encapsulate the messy reality of my own life, let alone say redemptive and beautiful things about my embodied reality as a woman, and I know that I'm not an outlier here. There is a service in the Book of Common Prayer which is rarely used any more but was once customary practice for all women who had been safely delivered of a child. *The Thanksgiving of Women After Childbirth*, known as *The Churching of Women*, gets a bad rap because it's seen as an archaic hangover from a time where women's post-natal bodies required the mediation of a priest to be socially acceptable before the community and God, but this is a simplistic reading of a history that is far more complex.[6] The service isn't unproblematic, by any means, but it was born out of an era of horrendous maternal mortality rates, and so it incorporates a sensitive pragmatism around the intersection of life and death. The Church of England has not authorized any other liturgy that performs the same function; that of centring the woman who has laboured, always at great physical cost and sometimes, even in this modern world of medical advancement, been brought to the brink of death. We are left with liturgies that celebrate the arrival of a child with no space offered in which to honour the mixed feelings of women who may be suffering birth trauma, or a worse tragedy. There is no space to come before God and the church and name publicly that the snares of death and the pains of hell had hold of us. We were in misery, but God helped us and preserved us.[7] We survived, but we are not whole.

If we're seeking more openness and less shame around meno-pause and midlife in the church, we must resist the temptation to speak of these things with a triumphalist overtone, which neglects to honour the shadow side. Yes, midlife can be enrich-ing and menopause has the potential to be a site of flourishing, and it's good for the church to celebrate that, but space must also be made for those for whom this isn't the case.

Like menopause, childbirth is a natural process and yet it is still the most violent thing that's ever happened to me. The water and blood that gushed from Jesus' side has always made perfect sense to me because childbirth included the free flow-ing of both these things. The viscous fluid that burst from me with an audible pop and splashed onto my bare toes, warm and salty, filling the air with a loamy, fecund scent. The blood that followed, dark red and less alarming than the scarlet fluid that came afterwards from my torn flesh. The guttural, watery cry of my newborn child recalling the death rattle I heard at the bedside of my dying grandfather. An arresting juxtaposition that testifies to the truth that 'In the midst of life, we are in death.'[8] Women have always known the nexus of life and death. We see it every day.

Women don't experience life in a straight line. We move in circles and spirals.[9] The linear concept of time in our modern world is one that isn't natural to us, because women have had to divorce ourselves from our bodily reality as a consequence of joining the workforce. In other words, the price we paid for equality was asserting that our biology wasn't a factor in disqualifying us from the public sphere, but in practice this has meant pretending that it doesn't impact on us at all. It would serve women far better if we were able to participate in the world while also acknowledging that we have needs that might be more suited to a different way of being.

A notion of time that doesn't allow for adequate rest or recuperation when we bleed, when we gestate, when we labour, when we go through the process to stop bleeding, is one that doesn't serve women well. It still bakes my brain that a woman can rise at the crack of dawn, undertake an hour's commute, work a twelve-hour shift while wearing a restrictive, tight uniform, all while bleeding copiously and coping with the pain of a uterus contracting like a bucking bronco, and must pretend that *it's not happening*. A culture of busyness and the pressure to always be doing is not the way of cyclical time, which prioritizes natural periods of rest and slowing down. It's not the way of women.

Since this is the way of the world, and it's not likely to change any time soon, we must find ways and practices for coping, and resisting that linear pull whenever we can. Not least of which is recognizing that a cyclical view of time is one that offers up theological truths. The waxing and waning of our wombs, and the cyclical nature of this process, means we confront many tiny deaths over a lifetime. It means that blood is not just a fluid of violence or loss, it is also one of regeneration and relief. A linear reading of the story of Jesus would have us proclaim that the cross and the resurrection are at opposite ends of a continuum,[10] where death is in the past and new life is something to look forward to in the future. This is a worthy view of redemption and one that I wish I could believe in, but my own experiences tell a different truth. That in the midst of life we can still be in death, that the two frequently rub up against one another, and that resurrection can carry echoes of the cross. This is a paradigm of hope for people suffering with depression and trauma, one that does not shrink from naming the darkness nor try to pretty it up to deny pain and loss.

In honouring the cyclical movement of time, I want to start where we began when we set off on our journey together, by returning to the book of Ruth. This short story, told in four acts, is part of the Megilloth, or the Five Small Scrolls, which also includes Esther, Ecclesiastes, Song of Songs and Lamentations. In Judaism, each book is associated with a Jewish festival, with Shavuot assigned to Ruth, which we know in the Christian faith as Pentecost, the day when the disciples of Jesus were visited by the Holy Spirit.[11] It's a simple story of two widows; a young woman who has hope (Ruth) and an older woman who knows only despair (Naomi). Among its themes are bereavement, displacement and steadfastness, and it shows how it's possible to seek and find new life despite depression and trauma.

The narrative begins by introducing Naomi, who fled her homeland of Judea due to famine, accompanied by her husband and two sons. They settled in neighbouring Moab, and the sons married Moabite women. Fast forward ten years and the husband and sons are all dead. Naomi is now thrice bereaved, a woman alone in the world without a man, without a dowry, without an inheritance, without youth, without hope. She refers to herself as 'the dead and me' (1.8).[12] When she left Judea as a young woman she was full of life, expectation, and hope: 'I went away full,' she says, 'but the LORD has brought me back empty' (1.21). She decides that her story will end where it started, in her hometown of Bethlehem, where she will return empty of everything other than the trauma that remains with her.

Naomi's only family in Moab are her daughters-in-law, Ruth and Orpah. Three women, alone in the world without male protection. Her daughters-in-law choose to go with her, but through the course of the journey they find themselves taking different paths. One woman goes back. One goes forward. One sinks into despair.[13] Ruth decides to stick with Naomi, and her words to her mother-in-law, 'Where you go, I will go', are the motif that runs through my reflections in this book, words that I've used as a declaration that the menopause wilderness will eventually be crossed by all women who bleed. On Ruth's lips these words are a promise of friendship, loyalty and devotion, a direct contrast to the competitiveness and jealousy in the warped connection between Hagar and Sarah. Naomi and Ruth demonstrate how redemptive the relationship between women can be when we trust in one another.

Naomi and Ruth are representatives of the territories they belong to,[14] so a reading of the book of Ruth can be understood as a story about the relationship between Israel and Moab, primarily considering the question, can outsiders be welcomed into the Jewish faith? It also poses questions outside this narrow sphere, such as how we welcome the foreigner and the migrant, and how we handle difference.

Through the lens of menopause, this story is about the interaction between generations, of a daughter-in-law and her mother-in-law. We're not told their ages, but it's not unreasonable to assume that Naomi is middle-aged, perhaps around fifty; she's raised sons to adulthood but since women were commonly married during their teens, this would still mean she's not what we would think of as old. Her words to Ruth and Orpah hint that this might be the case:

> Even if I thought there was hope for me, even if I should have a husband tonight and bear sons, would you then wait until they were grown? (Ruth 1.12–13)

Those words, *even if*, speak of a faint, lingering physical possibility of fertility, because the reason Naomi cites for not being able to bear more children isn't her menopausal body, it's the fact that God's hand has turned against her (1.13). Naomi has given up, which is the very definition of depression and the essence of Holy Saturday. It is a place where people no longer dare to test the boundaries of hope by placing faith in the word *if*. It's a psychological dead-end and 'nothing can be imagined beyond it'.[15]

Naomi's despair is so complete that she gives herself a new name, Mara, which means bitterness, to signify her belief that she is forsaken (1.20–21). Depression is often characterized by this feeling and can lead to an emotional and physical retreat from normal life. The theme of withdrawal runs through the text; Naomi withdraws from Bethlehem, she withdraws from Moab, she withdraws from her daughters-in-law, and she withdraws from God. Rather than trying to prevent this mental retreat, Ruth chooses to come alongside Naomi in her despair, and offer the ministry of presence.

Most women, when asked what they want the church to do to accommodate or support them in their menopause, don't actually want the church to *do* anything at all. They just want to be able to have the freedom to name what's happening to them without feeling embarrassed or ashamed. They want to be held by the church like Jesus held the hand of the woman with fever or have a place to speak the whole truth, like the bleeding woman did. Most women just want to feel like they're not suffering alone. There's a lesson here for how absolute love is modelled, by partaking of someone's misery just by sitting beside them. Holy Saturday is God's demonstration to us that there is no place he won't go to be beside his children through their suffering. Like Naomi, God has also travelled to the regions of God-forsakenness,[16] and for the depressed and traumatized this is a thought that gives comfort when little else does.

The story of Ruth and Naomi also offers resurrection hope. Naomi, who left her home in Bethlehem during the fullness of youth, now returns empty accompanied by her youthful daughter-in-law, Ruth. Naomi sinks into the background while the younger woman takes centre stage in the bulk of the action. Ruth's a curiosity because she's a foreigner, but she's also undeniably of interest (and at risk of danger) because she's young and single.

Jewish Midrash on Ruth makes the extraordinary claim that 'everyone who saw her orgasmed',[17] which is a most inconvenient thing to happen, particularly if you're just popping to

Aldi to pick up some parsnips. In his study of Ruth, Padraig O'Tuama asks the question: 'What is it like to be a person whose presence in a place arouses all kinds of reactions in your onlookers?'[18] A question that could be answered by most teenage girls and young women. Without unpacking the outrageous claim about people climaxing at the sight of Ruth, it does remind me of what it's like to be in public in the company of my teenage daughters. It's impossible not to notice the male eyes that follow them about, the heads that swivel to watch them as they pass, and the men who slow their cars down and occasionally shout and whistle through open windows. It was the same for me when I was their age, until the day when it wasn't. Gradually, I wasn't young any more and I found that I'd become invisible, which at first was a jarring experience, but now I appreciate it for the freedom it affords me. My body isn't under scrutiny any more, in the way it was when I was younger, and this is truly a blessing. Like Naomi, I'm of lesser interest, with younger women carrying the burden of the male gaze, as Ruth does.

The story of Ruth and Naomi reminds me that the invisibility midlife women complain of at this time of life need not be a curse, but can be regarded as a gift. The extreme objectification of young women and girls has been normalized and encouraged in our culture and is something that 'distorts the visual significance of the female body'.[19] Against this fallen background, menopause as resurrection is an invitation for us to find new ways of seeing our bodies as worthy and inherently wonderful, even if they have lost value to certain areas of the wider culture, and by doing this we encourage the world to do the same.

St Augustine offers such a vision in *City of God*, where he imagines the sexed bodies of females as being 'part of a new beauty, one that will not excite the lust of the beholder'.[20] The guy *had issues*, clearly, but he hints at a vision of resurrection that involves body neutrality, where women will be free of the concerns of our sex. He sees a vision where lust won't be a factor, which Tina Beattie reframes as women not being seen any longer as sex objects: 'A joyful celebration of the female body in the eyes of God.'[21] We can hope that this vision also includes eyes that no longer objectify. This is, of course, one of the unexpected freedoms of midlife, but I would also like to hope that one day younger women can also share in it. (I also hope that Crewe Alexandra might one day win the FA Cup, but life has so far taught me that hoping ain't getting.)

There is a traditional happy ending; Ruth marries Boaz (a kinsman of Naomi) and they have a child, who grows up to be the grandfather of King David and so appears in the genealogy of Jesus. As we saw with Sarah, Naomi finds new life through the birth of a baby, who through Jewish custom will be her next-of-kin and the grandchild that she would have had. 'He shall be to you a restorer of life and a nourisher of your old age,' she's told by the women (4.15). Naomi ends where she started. In the recovery from trauma there are no truly happy endings. We will always live with what remains, happily, sadly ever after.

This is the testimony of Holy Saturday. A testimony of a love that endures, not in triumph or exaltation, but in sacred desolation,

It starts where it ends. With nothingness. With an echoing void. But if I listen closely, there it is: God is here. His spirit is with me. And in my pain, in my anger and in my loneliness, I lift up my heart. I lift it up to the Lord, and he teaches me how to carry it through water and blood.

Notes

1 Balthazar, Hans Urs von, 'Easter: He walked where there was no path' (an excerpt from the collection of Hans Urs von Balthasar's radio sermons entitled 'You Crown the Year with Your Goodness: Sermons Throughout the Liturgical Year', *Church Life Journal*, 13 April 2020, https://churchlifejournal.nd.edu/articles/easter-we-walked-where-there-was-no-path/ (accessed on 26.4.24).

2 Rambo, S., *Spirit of Trauma: A Theology of Remaining* (Louisville: Westminster John Knox Press, 2010, p. 73).

3 Stuart Townend and Keith Getty Copyright © 2001 Thankyou Music, https://www.songs@integritymusic.com (accessed 26.4.24).

4 Gunter, J., *The Menopause Manifesto: Own Your Health with Facts and Feminism* (London: Piatkus, 2021).

5 Gunter, *The Menopause Manifesto*.

6 If you're interested in the history of churching, I highly recommend Margaret Houlbrooke, *Rite Out of Time: A Study of the Churching of Women and Its Survival in the Twentieth Century* (Donington: Shaun Tyas, 2011). She uses church records and first-person accounts from women who participated in the churching service to paint a picture that differs from the simplistic narrative of religious coercion and sexism that's often used to describe it.

7 Psalm 116, one of the two psalm readings suggested in the churching service. The other is Psalm 127, which is more celebratory.

8 The Order for the Burial of the Dead, Book of Common Prayer.

9 Pearce, K., *The Moon Lodge: Remembering Sacred Rites of Passage in Daily Life* (published by Kirsty Pearce, 2022).

10 Rambo, *Spirit of Trauma* (p. 143).

11 Birch, B., Brueggemann, W., Fretheim, T. and Petersen, D., *A Theological Introduction to the Old Testament* (Nashville: Abingdon Press, 2005, 2nd edn, p. 452).

12 Weems, R. J., *Just a Sister Away: Understanding the Timeless Connection Between Women of Today and Women in the Bible* (New York: Hatchette, 2007, ebook).

13 Weems, *Just a Sister Away* (Loc 502).

14 Ó'Tuama, P. and Jordan, G., *Border and Belonging: The Book of Ruth, a Story for Our Times* (London: Canterbury Press, 2021).

15 Rambo, *Spirit of Trauma* (p. 73).

16 Rambo, *Spirit of Trauma* (p. 68).

17 Attributed to Rabbi Yochanan, in Ruth Rabbah, Chapter Four, quoted by Ó'Tuama, *Border and Belonging*.

18 Ó'Tuama and Jordan, *Border and Belonging*.

19 Beattie, T., *God's Mother, Eve's Advocate: A Marian Narrative of Women's Salvation* (London: Continuum, 2002, p. 155).

20 St Augustine, *City of God*, Bk 22, Ch. 17, quoted in Beattie, *God's Mother* (p. 54).

21 Beattie, *God's Mother* (p. 54).

We part ways at the crossroads on the seventh day

Crumbs in the wilderness

We've arrived at a place at the edge of the wilderness, a border-land to the unknown. From here we can see the past behind us, the future before us, and a present that's ours to claim for our own. Here we make our choices and say our goodbyes.

Ahead lies transformation. If I look forwards into the distance to my mother, I can see something of what that change might be. If I look behind me to my daughters, I see what once was and what was lost. And if this small taster of the wilderness has taught me anything at all, it's that I can't go back. I can only move forward, into the uncertainty of a certain outcome: this is my midlife. Praise God that I've made it this far. The meaning can only be found ahead of me, in you, God.

We women who have spent time together in the wilderness have been changed by the journey, which is what any stint in the wilderness should do. We've wrestled with demons. We've laughed with angels. We will never be the same again. We carry scars from the experience, but we've emerged stronger, wiser, more settled than ever before. We are wide awake and ready for the next adventure that God has in store for us. For some, myself among them, the journey is only just beginning and we feel happier knowing we're not travelling by ourselves. We have our sisters for company, young and old, and we must never stop knowing one another. We pray that the church will come along with us, to honour our journey and to mark it as sacred. We have hope that we will never again have to struggle alone.

Back at the crossroads, it's now just me and the girl. All is strangely peaceful.

'It'll be OK,' she says, gently squeezing my hand.

'And when it's not?' I ask.

'Then I'll always be with you, day after day after day, right up to the end of the age.'

She releases my hand and slowly kneels down on the ground. With her finger she writes a message in the dirt, written with the rounded, whirly letters of a child.

I lower my eyes and I read the words the girl etched into the dry earth:

God was here.

Through every step. Through every hard moment. Through every long, dark night and every hot, exhausting day. Through the heat and the hard climbs. Through the rage. Through the fever and the fog. Through it all. We were never really lost, and we were never once forgotten. We were sustained. We were listened to. We were guided. We were understood. We were encouraged when we were tired and comforted when we despaired. And when we lay down at night to lie sleepless and aching, God lay beside us so that we wouldn't be alone. We were shown the way.

A faint sigh in my ear says, 'Woman, I say to you, arise!' I look back to the ground and the small form of the girl has gone. I smile, breathe in long and deep, and take one step forwards, away from the crossroads and on out into the wilderness.

Where you go, I will go.

She never left us. She never will.

A postcard from the wilderness 2

I've spent the past year with some amazing women. They've kept me hopeful when I've been exhausted and have despaired. They've sustained me when I wanted to give up. They've inspired me when I needed a boost. They've kept me company when I've felt alone. Their names are Sarah, Elizabeth, Mary and Naomi. Some of their names are unknown to me though I know their stories so well. They are a bleeding woman, a dead girl, a feverish relative. The record they left has been pinned up above my desk and I've looked at them every day. These women of God have kept me going and they feel like dear friends. The stories of women really do matter, and it's been a privilege to help tell them.

The command of Jesus to get up and serve him is not a simple one. Some of us, for various reasons, are unable to serve in the ways we thought we'd been called to. Like the journey through the wilderness, obstacles might block our path or we may have to go round the long way to get to where we thought we were going. We might not arrive at our destination at all. Life might take us elsewhere. Still, we serve because that is what Jesus has commissioned us to do.

The woman who nurtures a lifelong call to preach but belongs to a church where she is barred from doing so, and yet is so filled by the Spirit of God that she proclaims his word every time she opens her mouth because it is always on her lips. The woman who once was a Sunday school teacher, but due to disability and illness can no longer leave the house, so now she shows Jesus to the nurses who come into her home to take care of her. The woman who has lost a fulfilling career in law due to mental health issues, but who now has found new life and purpose by serving in the sacristy at her local church, every

Sunday. The woman who was called to be a priest but who suffered a traumatic breakdown that pushed her to the point of suicide and so no longer works in parish-based ministry, but who started writing this book as a way to heal from that experience.

I pray that my words serve you well. I pray you feel comforted. I pray you feel less alone. I pray you feel proud of who you are and of who you've been. I pray you feel excited about who you're becoming. I pray you never lose hope. I pray you never stop seeking God with all your heart and all your mind, and I pray you find purpose and wonder in the meaning of midlife.

This is our wakening. This is our time. Let's grab those tambourines and get busy waking up the church.

Waking the women:
A litany of menopause

We menopausal women of the church, pray to you our God, who was born of a woman. Who was fed by a woman. Who was raised by a woman. Who ministered alongside women. Who was comforted by women. Who wept with women.
Hear our prayer.

We follow in the footsteps of the women of your word, and we take comfort from their stories. Share with us the gifts that were given to them and command us to arise.
Sarah, who gave birth to laughter after knowing despair.
Call: Women, God says to us, Arise.
Response: Wake up, Women. Today is a new dawn.

Elizabeth, who gave birth to joy after a lifetime of patience.
Call: Women, God says to us, Arise.
Response: Wake up, Women. Today is a new dawn.

The bleeding woman, who showed great faith and courage in telling the whole truth without shame.
Call: Women, God says to us, Arise.
Response: Wake up, Women. Today is a new dawn.

The girl who you raised from the dead and who reminds us that there is always new life to be found in you.
Call: Women, God says to us, Arise.
Response: Wake up, Women. Today is a new dawn.

Peter's mother-in-law, who you healed and enabled to serve.
Call: Women, God says to us, Arise.
Response: Wake up, Women. Today is a new dawn.

The forgotten and lost deaconesses of your church, who you
equipped, emboldened and enabled.
Call: Women, God says to us, Arise.
Response: Wake up, Women. Today we serve the Lord.

Stay close to us. Give us the strength to obey your command
to wake up to the gifts that this new season brings us. Show us
the meaning of midlife.
Amen.

Bibliography

Unless explicitly stated otherwise, all biblical references are from the NRSV Anglicized Edition.

Atwood, M., *Eating Fire: Selected Poetry 1965–1995* (London: Virago, 2010).

Austen, J., *Pride and Prejudice* (London: Penguin Classics, first published in 1813, this edition 1996).

Balthazar, Hans Urs von, 'Easter: He walked where there was no path' (an excerpt from the collection of Hans Urs von Balthasar's radio sermons, 'You Crown the Year with Your Goodness: Sermons Throughout the Liturgical Year', *Church Life Journal*, 13 April 2020, https://churchlifejournal.nd.edu/articles/easter-we-walked-where-there-was-no-path/ (accessed on 26.4.24).

Beattie, T., *God's Mother, Eve's Advocate: A Marian Narrative of Women's Salvation* (London: Continuum, 2002).

Birch, B., Brueggemann, W., Fretheim, T. and Petersen, D., *A Theological Introduction to the Old Testament*, 2nd edition (Nashville: Abingdon Press, 2005).

Bridges, W., *Managing Transitions: Making the Most of Change* (London: Nicholas Brealey Publishing, 2017).

Bridges Johns, C., *The Seven Transforming Gifts of Menopause* (Ada: Brazos Press, 2020).

Brown, L. Mikel and Gilligan, C., *Meeting at the Crossroads: Women's Psychology and Girls' Development* (Cambridge: Harvard University Press, 1992).

Bruce, K. and Shercliff, L., *Out of the Shadows: Preaching the Women of the Bible* (London: SCM Press, 2021).

Cocksworth, A., Starr, R. and Burns, S. (eds), with Nicola Slee, *From the Shores of Silence: Conversations in Feminist Practical Theology* (London: SCM Press, 2023).

Curtice, J., Clery, E., Perry, J., Phillips M. and Rahim, N. (eds), 'British Social Attitudes: The 36th Report' (London: The National Centre for Social Research, 2019), https://natcen.ac.uk/publications/british-social-attitudes-36 (accessed 26.4.24).

Davis, E., *Getting Involved with God: Rediscovering the Old Testament* (Lanham: Rowman & Littlefield Publishers, Inc., 2001).

Eclair, J., *Older and Wider: A Survivor's Guide to the Menopause* (London: Quercus, 2020).

Gaffney, W., *Womanist Midrash: A Reintroduction to the Women of the Torah and the Throne* (Louisville: Westminster John Knox Press, 2017).

Gittoes, J., 'Her bleeding stopped: The embodied borderland of the menopause', http://juliegittoes.blogspot.com/2021/10/her-bleeding-stopped-embodied.html (accessed 26.4.24).

Gooder, P., *The Parables* (London: Canterbury Press, 2020).

Greer, G., *The Change: Women, Ageing and The Menopause* (London: Bloomsbury, 2019 revised edition).

Gunter, J., *The Menopause Manifesto: Own your Health with Facts and Feminism* (London: Piatkus, 2021).

Handley MacMath, T., 'Interview: Cheryl Bridges Johns, Professor of Spiritual Renewal', *Church Times*, 23 October 2020, https://www.churchtimes.co.uk/articles/2020/23-october/features/interviews/interview-cheryl-bridges-johns-professor-of-spiritual-renewal (accessed 26.4.24).

Heppenstall, A., *The Book of Uncommon Prayer* (Buxhall: Kevin Meyhew, 2015).

Hicks, P., 'Kate Moss at Fifty: Why she is finding ageing harder than her own Mossy Posse', *The Independent*, 13 January 2024, https://www.independent.co.uk/life-style/kate-moss-50-mossy-posse-primrose-hill-midlife-b2476887.html (accessed 26.4.24).

Lang, Z., Reynolds Losin, E., Asher, Y., Koban, L. and Wager, T., 'Gender Biases in Estimation of Others' Pain', *Journal of Pain*, 22(9), September 2021, https://www.jpain.org/article/S1526-5900(21)00035-3/fulltext (accessed 26.4.24).

Levine, A.-J. and Zvi Brettler, M. (eds), *The Jewish Annotated New Testament, New Revised Standard Bible Translation* (Oxford: Oxford University Press, 2011).

Levitin, D. J., *The Changing Mind: A Neuroscientist's Guide to Ageing Well* (London: Penguin, 2021).

Low, M., *God, I'm Angry! Anger, Forgiveness, and the Psalms of Vengeance* (Carlisle: Langham Global Library, 2023).

Luther, M., *What Luther Says: An Anthology*, Vol. 1, compiled by Ewald M. Plass (St Louis: Concordia, 1959, entry nos 28, 29).

Mattern, S., *The Slow Moon Climbs: The Science, History and Meaning of Menopause* (Princeton: Princeton University Press, 2019).

McLean, A., *Confessions of a Menopausal Woman: Everything You Wanted to Know but Were Afraid to Ask* (London: Bantam Press, 2018).

Newsom, C. A. and Ringe, S. H. (eds), *The Women's Bible Commentary* (London: SPCK, 1992).

Opelt, A. Held, *Holy Unhappiness: God, Goodness and the Myth of the Blessed Life* (New York: Hachette Book Group, 2023).

Ó'Tuama, P. and Jordan, G., *Border and Belonging: The Book of Ruth, a Story for our Times* (London: Canterbury Press, 2021).

Pearce, K., *The Moon Lodge: Remembering Sacred Rites of Passage in Daily Life* (published by Kirsty Pearce, 2022).

Rambo, S., *Spirit of Trauma: A Theology of Remaining* (Louisville: Westminster John Knox Press, 2010).

Rogers, A., 'Voice, Play, and a Practice of Ordinary Courage in Girls' and Women's Lives', *Harvard Educational Review*, 63(3), 1 September 1993.

Slee, N., *The Book of Mary* (London: SPCK, 2007).

Slee, N., 'Writing like a Woman: In search of a feminist theological poetics', in D'Costa, G., et al., *Making Nothing Happen: Five Poets Explore Faith and Spirituality* (Farnham: Ashgate, 2014).

Smith, V., *Hags: The Demonisation of Middle-Aged Women* (London: Fleet, 2023).

Steinke, D., *Flash Count Diary: A New Story about the Menopause* (Edinburgh: Canongate Books, 2019).

Storkey, E., 'The Bleeding Woman', https://www.elainestorkey.com/woman-alive-series/ (accessed 26.4.24).

Swan, L., *The Forgotten Desert Mothers: Sayings, Lives and Stories of Early Christian Women* (New York: Paulist Press, 2001).

Thorp, C., 'How Daniel Craig became the fittest 50-year-old on the planet', *Men's Journal*, 20 April 2020, https://www.mensjournal.com/health-fitness/how-daniel-craig-became-the-fittest-50-year-old-on-the-planet (accessed 26.4.24).

Trzebiatowska, M. and Bruce, S., *Why are Women More Religious than Men?* (Oxford: Oxford University Press, 2012).

VanOsdol, J., 'Talitha Cum: The raising up of Women and Girls to Overcome Violence', in *Overcoming Violence: Churches Seeking Reconciliation and Peace* (World Council of Churches, 2011), http://www.overcomingviolence.org/en/resources-dov/wcc-resources/documents/bible-studies/talitha-cum-the-raising-up-of-women-and-girls-to-overcome-violence.html (accessed 26.4.24).

Weems, R. J., *Just a Sister Away: Understanding the Timeless Connection Between Women of Today and Women in the Bible* (New York: Hatchette, 2007, ebook).

Wesley, J., 'Upon Our Lord's Sermon on the Mount', Sermon 22 in *The Works of John Wesley*, Vol. 5 (Grand Rapids: Zondervan, 1958, p. 264).

Wilk, K., *Perimenopower: Your Essential Guide to the Change Before the Change* (London: Orion Spring, 2020).

Wright, T., *Mark for Everyone* (London: SPCK, 2001).

Young-Somers, D., 'It Says what?!', zoom conversation hosted by JW3 London, https://www.youtube.com/watch?v=mToldJ8hQ7M&t=263s (accessed 26.4.24).

Index of Bible References

Index of Subjects

anger 3, 12, 23, 34, 35,
  41–52, 94, *see also* rage
anxiety 5, 58, 75, 78

bleeding
  normal menstrual 9, 10,
    12–14, 23, 89
  abnormal/heavy 17–20, 56,
    58, 92, 98, 100
brain fog 5, 62

depression 16, 34, 70, 86–7,
  90–2, *see also* trauma

fertility xv, 37, 59, 76–7, 80,
  84–5, 91

hair
  excess 57, 28, 81
  grey xvi, 9, 22, 39

Hormone Replacement
  Therapy (HRT) 6, 56
hot flushes 5, 8, 57–61, 75

insomnia 5

rage xiii, xvi, 5, 13, 15,
  41–2, 45–51

sex drive 79–80

trauma 57, 86–8, 90, 92, 94

vaginal dryness xi, 75, 79

weight gain 2, 16, 57, 72